Banking 2050: Reimagining Finance in a Decentralized, Digital World

Author Information – Amulya Mishra

Amulya Mishra is a proficient author and banking specialist with a profound interest in economic theory and storytelling. Amulya's work is grounded on a robust academic and practical foundation, since he possesses an MBA in Banking and Finance, a graduate degree in Accounting, and other banking certifications.

Amulya was born and nurtured in Patna, and her journey has been characterized by discipline, curiosity, and creativity. His works, encompassing both fiction and non-fiction, exemplify his extensive intellect and insatiable curiosity. His non-fiction writings, such as "Bond: A Barometer of the Economy" and his analysis of the G20 Presidency, illustrate his capacity to distill complex topics into engaging narratives, encompassing issues ranging from the intricacies of cryptocurrencies to the dynamics of international financial instruments.

His conceived universes, meanwhile, are equally enthralling. His gripping horror novel "Mirror Mirror Mirror" showcases a chilling imagination, while his forthcoming work "Superpower 2050" appears to be a formidable geopolitical analysis.

Amulya has been writing for as long as he can recall and is inherently a writer. He perceives writing as a vocation that intertwines facts and emotions, reason and wonder, rather than simply a craft.

This piece signifies yet another step in his evolving literary career. Amulya asserts that his words exert a profound and substantial influence on you, irrespective of your purpose for being here— be it inspiration, exhilaration, or reflection. I value your support of him on this trip, and I trust this endeavor will offer you pleasure and heightened engagement.

This book refrains from endorsing any sort of prejudice or bias toward persons, institutions, or nations. It seeks to provide insights into the possible trajectories of global finance by 2050. In this era of hyper-connectivity, the significance of technical ethics, economic inclusiveness, and human-centric innovation is paramount.

All views expressed below are exclusively those of the author and aim to stimulate critical analysis and informed dialogue. The opinions expressed do not represent the official position of financial institutions or regulatory authorities.

PREFACE

"Banking 2050: Reimagining Finance in a Decentralized, Digital World" emerged from a profound aspiration to comprehend and elucidate the future trajectory of the financial landscape. As banking experiences one of the most profound shifts in history—characterized by digital currencies, decentralized systems, and artificial intelligence—it is essential to reconceptualize finance not merely as an industry, but as a catalyst that influences societies.

This book examines potentialities. It encapsulates the potential landscape of finance by 2050 and outlines how we, as global citizens, should ready ourselves for that future. It links historical lessons with prospective insights, providing readers from many experiences a thorough perspective on the forthcoming journey.

I encourage you to engage with this book with inquisitiveness and receptivity. May the data, projections, and insights herein enable you to transcend current constraints and envision future advancements.

May this voyage be illuminating, empowering, and, above all, intellectually stimulating.

ACKNOWLEDGEMENTS

I would like to express my deepest gratitude to my family, especially my wife, Sheetal, whose unwavering love and support have been my strength throughout the writing of this book. Her encouragement during moments of doubt gave me the clarity and determination to keep moving forward.

To my beloved parents—my first teachers and my lifelong inspiration—thank you for your sacrifices, wisdom, and the values you instilled in me. Your blessings and faith in my journey have guided me every step of the way.

I also wish to thank my colleagues and peers in the banking and financial sector, especially those in Goa, who fostered an environment that allowed ideas to flourish and this work to take shape.

Spiritually, I bow in gratitude to the divine presence that has illuminated my path during challenging times. I offer humble thanks to Haji Ali Dargah for the strength and serenity I have found there, to Shirdi Sai Baba for continuous guidance, and to all the divine forces who watched over me throughout this journey. Their blessings have been a silent but powerful force behind this book.

This work is also a result of years of reflection, learning, and persistent inquiry. I thank all my teachers and professors who nurtured my curiosity and gave me the tools to think critically and write meaningfully.

Above all, I thank the Almighty for the gift of life, knowledge, and purpose. May this book serve its readers well and contribute to a future shaped by wisdom, innovation, and integrity.

Introduction: Banking—The Invisible Engine

Every time you tap your phone to pay for a coffee, take out a loan to buy a house, or transfer funds across borders, you are engaging with a financial system shaped by centuries of evolution, conquest, crisis, and innovation. Yet most of us never see its inner workings.

Banks are more than money warehouses—they are the beating heart of modern civilization. From the ancient grain banks of Babylon to high-speed algorithmic trading in New York and Shanghai, banking has not just adapted to the times—it has shaped them.

In an era where AI predicts our spending habits, central banks issue digital currencies, and fintech startups challenge age-old institutions, understanding how global banking systems function is no longer optional. It's essential.

This book aims to take you on a comprehensive yet accessible journey through the world's banking ecosystems. You'll discover how different countries structure their banks, why crises erupt with little warning, and how money quietly wields power behind political decisions and public policy.

We will explore banking models from America's Wall Street to Kenya's mobile money revolution. We'll dive into digital transformation, ethical banking, and the threats that loom over global finance—cyberattacks, pandemics, and artificial intelligence.

This is not a book just for economists or bankers. It's for every global citizen who wants to understand the gears turning beneath their daily transactions. Whether you're an entrepreneur, student, policymaker, or just curious about the future of money—this book is your map to the vaults of global financial power.

Let's unlock the doors.

Chapter 1: The Disruption Timeline

The FinTech surge and Big Tech's entry

Collapse of traditional models post-2030

Transition to real-time, digital-first finance.

Chapter 2: Banks Become Ecosystems

Banking-as-a-service (BaaS)

Platformization and APIs

From monoliths to modular ecosystems

Case studies: IndiaStack, Ant Group, Open Banking in Europe

Chapter 3: The Rise of Intelligent Finance

AI and ML in wealth management, credit, and compliance

Emotion-aware financial tools

Quantum computing in financial modeling

Future of algorithmic banking

Chapter 4: The New Currency Order

CBDCs and national digital currencies

The integration of stablecoins and crypto

Programmable money and smart contracts

DeFi 2.0: Decentralized finance at scale

Chapter 5: Financial Inclusion Reimagined

Digital identity revolution

Biometric wallets and satellite-based connectivity

Rural banking without banks

Chapter 1: The Disruption Timeline

As we cast our eyes toward the mid-21st century, we must first look back at the chaotic, catalytic decades that preceded it. The disruption of banking wasn't a single event but a layered series of tremors, each shaking the financial bedrock until the old world crumbled to make way for a smarter, faster, more inclusive ecosystem. The story begins in the 2020s—a decade marked by pandemics, technological acceleration, and a global awakening to the limitations of legacy banking.

The 2020s: The Great Digital Acceleration

The COVID-19 pandemic proved to be more than a health crisis—it was a forcing function. In months, digital transformation accelerated at a pace previously expected to take a decade. Banks scrambled to serve clients remotely. Physical branches shuttered by the thousands. Contactless payments, mobile wallets, and neo-banks became the default for billions.

The pandemic also exposed systemic inequalities in access. In emerging economies, millions remained unbanked. Yet at the same time, grassroots FinTechs from Africa to Southeast Asia bloomed, leapfrogging traditional infrastructure and building mobile-first financial ecosystems tailored for underserved populations.

Meanwhile, the Western banking system faced existential questions. Legacy core systems buckled under demand. Compliance costs soared. Customer expectations, influenced by Big Tech experiences, skyrocketed. The result? An unprecedented wave of consolidation, partnerships with FinTechs, and regulatory sandboxes designed to accelerate innovation without compromising systemic stability.

The 2030s: The Platformization of Finance

By 2030, a clear paradigm shift had taken hold: banks were no longer seen as institutions but as platforms. Banking-as-a-Service (BaaS) models proliferated, allowing brands—retailers, telcos, even social media platforms—to embed financial services directly into their ecosystems. Banking became invisible, ambient, and ubiquitous.

Open banking regulations had evolved into open finance standards, enabling customers to port their entire financial footprint across providers. APIs became the new competitive edge. Those who failed to adapt became utilities, offering commoditized services beneath slick FinTech wrappers.

At the same time, Big Tech's incursion into finance was both welcomed and feared. Amazon Bank, ApplePay+, and MetaCredit introduced frictionless, AI-powered banking, backed by data ecosystems far richer than any bank could dream of. Regulators responded with firewalls, but the genie was out of the bottle.

Simultaneously, decentralized finance (DeFi) began maturing. Once the domain of crypto enthusiasts, DeFi protocols offered real alternatives to lending, trading, and asset management—without intermediaries. The early 2030s saw the first sovereign DeFi partnerships, legitimizing the ecosystem.

The 2040s: The Age of Intelligent, Autonomous Finance

The next decade witnessed the rise of hyper-personalized, autonomous banking. AI agents, embedded in personal devices and digital identities, began managing finances proactively—paying bills, reallocating investments, and optimizing tax outcomes in real time.

Quantum computing, now commercialized, revolutionized risk modeling and fraud detection. Banks could simulate millions of scenarios in seconds, offering dynamic pricing and predictive interventions. Insurance, credit, and savings were no longer sold—they were algorithmically curated.

Central Bank Digital Currencies (CBDCs) were now operational in over 100 countries, creating a new global financial fabric. Payments became instant, programmable, and traceable. Monetary policy execution shifted from macro to micro, with central banks injecting incentives directly into individual wallets.

Meanwhile, ESG-aligned finance became the default. Carbon taxes, sustainability-linked loans, and environmental credit ratings shaped how capital flowed. Banks weren't just lenders—they were climate actors, embedding sustainability into every transaction.

A Tectonic Transformation

What makes this timeline extraordinary is not just the speed of change but its depth. Finance transitioned from a permissioned, institution-centric industry to an open, intelligent, and often autonomous network. The power no longer rested in skyscrapers—it flowed through code, connectivity, and credibility.

Yet, for all its advances, this evolution also brought risks: algorithmic bias, data monopolies, cyber vulnerabilities, and a redefinition of trust. As we enter the 2050s, the challenge isn't just to build better banks but to build a better banking future for everyone.

And so begins our journey.

Chapter 2: Banks Become Ecosystems

By the early 2030s, the fundamental structure of banking had evolved into something far more organic and integrated: a system of interconnected platforms rather than monolithic institutions. Banks, once towering beacons of centralized control, had transformed into dynamic ecosystems. These ecosystems allowed for seamless collaboration, innovation, and service delivery through digital interfaces, application programming interfaces (APIs), and decentralized protocols. The shift from closed institutions to open platforms wasn't just technological—it was cultural, philosophical, and economic.

The Rise of Banking-as-a-Service (BaaS)

Banking-as-a- Service emerged as one of the defining features of this transformation. Instead of owning the end-to-end customer relationship, traditional banks began offering their infrastructure as a service to third parties. Startups, telecom companies, e-commerce platforms, and even governments started building financial services atop the backbones of established banks.

This meant that consumers could access banking functions—savings, loans, payments, and insurance—within apps they used daily. A farmer in Kenya could get a microloan via a mobile agriculture app. A teenager in Tokyo could invest in global stocks via a social media account. Banking became modular, programmable, and contextually embedded in digital life.

From Pipelines to Platforms

Historically, banks operated like pipelines: linear systems where value flowed from deposits to loans to profits. But in the new era, banks operate as platforms—curated ecosystems where multiple participants create and capture value.

Think of a modern bank more like a digital app store than a vault. Customers can access third-party budgeting tools, ESG scoring systems, investment robo-advisors, and even tokenized assets—all through one interface. Banks no longer needed to build every service themselves. Instead, they curated ecosystems of trusted partners.

This model expanded rapidly due to the maturity of open banking frameworks. Regulatory mandates forced financial institutions to share customer data—securely and with consent— with licensed third parties. This unleashed a wave of innovation and specialization, where niche players could thrive without owning the entire financial stack.

The Global Spread of Open Finance

Open Banking, pioneered in the EU and UK, evolved into global Open Finance standards by the mid-2030s. These frameworks expanded beyond bank accounts to include insurance, pensions, mortgages, and crypto holdings. Every citizen could aggregate their financial life into a single interface and switch providers with the ease of changing mobile plans.

Emerging markets like Brazil, India, and Nigeria led in implementation, leapfrogging legacy models. India's unified payment interface (UPI), Aadhaar digital identity, and account aggregator framework allowed banks and FinTechs to build expansive ecosystems on a shared digital public infrastructure. By 2040, over a billion Indians managed their finances through personalized, intelligent, multi-provider platforms.

Latin American and African nations adopted similar models, spurred by the flexibility and resilience of open ecosystems. Local FinTechs built culturally tailored products that understood local needs—from remittances to crop insurance—more effectively than global banks ever could.

Embedded Finance Everywhere

Banking in 2050 isn't a destination—it's an embedded layer in everything. Buying a car, subscribing to online content, booking a vacation, or managing household utilities—each transaction is underpinned by invisible financial tools.

E-commerce platforms offer credit and dynamic pricing. Streaming services recommend savings products based on viewing habits. Smart refrigerators negotiate grocery credits based on loyalty rewards. In this world, finance flows like electricity—quiet, constant, vital.

The Role of Digital Identity and Trust

For ecosystems to thrive, trust needed redefinition. Traditional KYC (Know Your Customer) models proved inadequate in a world of decentralized access and instant onboarding. Digital identity systems based on biometrics and blockchain allowed individuals to port verified credentials across platforms.

Zero-knowledge proofs and privacy-preserving technologies enabled customers to verify attributes (like age or income) without revealing sensitive data. This underpinned a new trust architecture—dynamic, secure, and user-controlled.

Risks and Regulatory Reflections

Ecosystems brought incredible innovation—but also risks. Concentration of power among platform gatekeepers, dependency on opaque algorithms, and interoperability issues presented challenges. Regulators had to rethink antitrust frameworks, systemic risk definitions, and consumer protection in environments where the 'bank' could be a social network, a gaming company, or a ride-sharing app.

Some regions responded with "Digital Financial Constitutions"—legal blueprints defining rights, responsibilities, and standards for ecosystem participants. These included rights to data portability, redress mechanisms, and algorithmic transparency.

Conclusion: A Living System

By 2050, banks are no longer closed institutions—they are living systems. They adapt, evolve, and collaborate across networks. Their success is measured not just by profits, but by their ability to connect, empower, and co-create with others.

This transformation—from pipelines to platforms, from institutions to ecosystems—is not the end of banking. It is its renaissance.

Chapter 3: The Rise of Intelligent Finance

By 2050, finance has entered a phase that is less about infrastructure and more about intelligence. Data-driven decisions, predictive algorithms, and autonomous systems have become foundational in personal banking, corporate finance, and global monetary policy. The era of Intelligent Finance marks the convergence of Artificial Intelligence (AI),

Machine Learning (ML), Quantum Computing, and real-time analytics, radically transforming how money is managed, moved, and multiplied.

From Reactive to Proactive Finance

Traditionally, financial institutions operated reactively—processing applications, responding to risks, and adjusting strategies post-facto. Intelligent Finance flips this model on its head. Today, AI-driven systems anticipate needs, detect anomalies before they emerge, and initiate actions on behalf of users.

Consider a typical customer in 2050. Their AI financial assistant, integrated into their daily environment—from AR glasses to smart speakers—monitors income, expenses, market shifts, and personal goals in real time. Without needing to be prompted, it reallocates funds to optimize tax benefits, postpones discretionary payments during economic uncertainty, or suggests investment opportunities based on hyper-local trends.

These assistants are emotionally aware, adapting financial suggestions based on user mood, behavior, and psychological profiles. Finance has become personalized to a granular, human level.

The Role of Machine Learning in Banking Decisions

Machine learning now powers nearly every facet of banking:

Credit scoring integrates unconventional data—from social behavior to biometric patterns—to assess risk with far greater accuracy.

Fraud detection operates in milliseconds, flagging anomalies based on billions of data points, continually retraining models with each new case.

Customer service is managed by conversational AIs indistinguishable from human agents, fluent in multiple languages, and able to recall a customer's history across all channels.

This learning isn't static—it evolves. Models are continuously trained on anonymized global financial datasets, adjusting for macroeconomic trends, new types of fraud, and even changes in consumer psychology post-major events.

Quantum Finance: A New Paradigm

Perhaps the most groundbreaking leap came with the integration of quantum computing into financial modeling. In the early 2040s, breakthroughs in quantum stability allowed institutions to simulate multivariable economic scenarios with near-perfect accuracy.

Risk management, previously a field of probability and approximation, became an exercise in quantum certainty. Portfolios were optimized in real time across millions of variables—climate risk, geopolitical tensions, supply chain disruptions, and more.

This also enabled "quantum hedging"—new derivatives and insurance products designed to protect against black swan events by dynamically adjusting based on shifting quantum risk curves.

The Autonomous Bank

Banks themselves began to operate autonomously. Internal decisions—approvals, investments, compliance—are now handled by AI boards. These digital governance engines are programmed with organizational ethics, risk tolerance, and market strategy, making millions of micro-decisions daily.

Human executives focus on strategic vision, ethics alignment, and complex negotiations. In essence, humans moved up the chain—from operators to overseers.

Ethical Algorithms and Transparency

With great intelligence came great responsibility. A backlash against biased algorithms and opaque decision-making forced the industry to embed transparency and ethics into its models.

Explainable AI (XAI) became a regulatory requirement. Every automated decision—from loan denial to interest rate adjustment—must be explainable in plain language. Customers have the right to audit the logic behind major financial outcomes.

Ethics review boards, composed of ethicists, technologists, and citizen representatives, became common in major banks. These boards reviewed algorithmic behaviors, flagged unintended consequences, and ensured AI models aligned with evolving social values.

Adaptive, Real-Time Finance

One of the most exciting features of Intelligent Finance is its adaptability. Gone are the days of static budgets and fixed investment strategies. Today, financial plans are dynamic:

Savings goals adjust based on real-time economic forecasts.

Loan terms change based on borrower behavior.

Insurance premiums shift with live health or environmental data.

Even national monetary policy adapted. Central banks now use AI simulations to test policy changes across millions of personas and scenarios before implementation. Fiscal stimulus is targeted and personalized, injected into digital wallets based on predictive impact models.

Intelligent Finance for Businesses

Enterprises, too, reaped the benefits:

Treasury functions are AI-managed, optimizing liquidity and yield dynamically.

Supply chain finance is synchronized with IoT data, enabling real-time risk assessment.

Smart contracts execute autonomously, settling transactions based on satellite data, IoT sensors, or real-world event triggers.

Financial forecasting evolved from quarterly reports to live dashboards that simulate future balance sheets under countless scenarios.

The New Role of Financial Advisors

Humans didn't disappear from finance—they evolved with it. The financial advisor of 2050 is less a planner and more a behavioral coach. Supported by AI co-pilots, they help clients make emotionally aligned decisions, resolve conflicts between goals, and navigate life transitions with financial clarity.

Their job is not to predict the market—that's the AI's role—but to understand the human at the heart of it.

Conclusion: The Mind of Money

Finance in 2050 is no longer a system—it's a mind. Intelligent, adaptive, ethically guided, and deeply embedded into the lives of people and organizations. The future of banking isn't just smart—it's sentient in design, empathic in operation, and empowering in its intent.

This is the age of Intelligent Finance—and it has only just begun.

Chapter 4: Decentralized Dominance

By the mid-21st century, decentralized finance (DeFi) had transitioned from a fringe experiment into a dominant architectural pillar of the global financial system. What started as peer-to-peer lending and automated market makers evolved into a complex, resilient, and fully autonomous web of protocols rivaling—and in some cases replacing—traditional banking structures.

This chapter explores how decentralization moved from ideology to infrastructure, transforming power dynamics in banking, redefining ownership, and placing control back into the hands of individuals and communities.

The Rise of Protocol-Based Finance

DeFi in 2050 is not just an alternative—it is the standard. Hundreds of thousands of interoperable protocols now handle trillions of dollars in assets across lending, payments, insurance, derivatives, asset tokenization, and identity. These protocols are governed by decentralized autonomous organizations (DAOs), with decisions made via token-holder voting and algorithmic consensus.

The trust equation flipped: instead of relying on institutional credibility, users trust transparent code, cryptographic guarantees, and decentralized consensus. Smart contracts eliminated counterparty risk, middlemen, and delays, bringing unprecedented efficiency and security.

Tokenization of Everything

Virtually every asset class is now tokenized. Real estate, intellectual property, carbon credits, art, and even future revenue streams exist as digital tokens. These can be traded, fractionally owned, and used as collateral within the DeFi universe.

Ownership became granular. A 13-year-old in Ghana might own 0.0001% of a New York skyscraper and earn micro-dividends streamed in real time. Artists monetize their creations through self-governed NFT-based royalties, while farmers use tokenized harvest futures to secure funding months ahead.

This explosion of asset classes fueled liquidity and created vibrant, 24/7 global markets untethered from geography.

DAOs as the New Institutions

The DAO revolution upended organizational structure. Banks, investment firms, credit unions, and insurance companies evolved into algorithmically governed collectives. These entities are borderless, leaderless, and auditable by design.

Capital allocation is community-driven. Investment DAOs pool funds and vote on startup investments. Insurance DAOs use predictive oracles to dynamically adjust premiums and pay out claims. Reputation scores, not resumes, determine influence.

Governance token holders are the new stakeholders. They debate policy changes, vote on risk parameters, and earn yield not from passive savings but from active participation in governance.

Decentralized Identity and Reputation

Identity in a decentralized world is self-sovereign. Every individual maintains a wallet-based identity composed of cryptographic credentials, transaction history, and social attestations.

These decentralized identifiers (DIDs) enable access to services without revealing unnecessary personal data. A refugee can open a digital bank account with a biometric signature and a few blockchain-verified attestations—no passport required.

Reputation becomes portable. Whether applying for a microloan, joining a DAO, or buying insurance, your financial behavior is recorded immutably and permissionlessly, building trust without intermediaries.

Challenges and the Path to Maturity

Decentralization brought freedom—but also volatility. Early DeFi markets suffered from rug pulls, code exploits, and governance manipulation. Education, regulation, and security audits eventually matured the space.

Cross-chain interoperability solved liquidity fragmentation. Scalable layer-2 solutions reduced fees and improved speed. Decentralized arbitration platforms emerged to resolve disputes and enforce fairness.

Regulators embraced the challenge, creating "DeReg" frameworks—regulations embedded into protocols themselves. Instead of policing after-the-fact, compliance is proactive, encoded in the very architecture.

Central Banks and Programmable Stablecoins

Interestingly, central banks didn't disappear—they adapted. Most nations now issue programmable central bank digital currencies (CBDCs) that interact directly with DeFi protocols. These CBDCs come with embedded tax logic, compliance triggers, and expiration rules, enabling targeted stimulus and macroeconomic nudges.

Hybrid public-private protocols emerged where CBDCs coexist with algorithmic stablecoins. This ensured monetary stability while preserving the permissionless innovation of open finance.

Some countries—like Estonia, Singapore, and Uruguay—fully integrated CBDCs into DeFi rails, creating monetary systems with programmable logic and real-time economic telemetry.

Cultural and Societal Shifts

Decentralized finance reshaped how people think about money, power, and institutions. Financial literacy soared. Youth across the globe learned governance, economics, and technology by participating in real-world DAOs before finishing school.

Communities gained financial sovereignty. Indigenous groups tokenized land rights. Diasporas built global remittance DAOs. Marginalized voices finally had tools to shape their economic destiny without waiting for institutional permission.

Conclusion: A Distributed Future

Decentralization reimagined finance not as a service delivered to people but as a commons built by them. It flattened hierarchies, expanded access, and made finance an open-source endeavor.

In 2050, the question is no longer whether decentralization works—but how it can be governed fairly, scaled sustainably, and protected from co-option.

This is the era of Decentralized Dominance—a new foundation for the financial future of humanity.

Chapter 5: Embedded and Invisible Banking

As banking continues its evolution, the lines between financial services and daily life have all but disappeared. In 2050, banking is no longer a separate activity—it's embedded, ambient, and often invisible. Every transaction, decision, or interaction can carry a financial layer, seamlessly integrated into digital experiences.

This chapter explores how financial functionality has become woven into platforms, applications, and environments, transforming the delivery of financial services from a destination to an ever-present experience.

Embedded Finance: Banking Without Banks

Embedded finance refers to the seamless integration of financial services into non-financial platforms. Today, virtually every platform offers banking-like capabilities:

E-commerce platforms provide instant BNPL (Buy Now, Pay Later) powered by real-time credit scoring.

Ride-hailing apps manage driver income, taxes, and investments.

Social networks double as financial ecosystems, allowing tipping, loans, or investment in creators via smart contracts.

Fintech became a layer rather than a sector. Any digital product can now offer tailored financial services—payments, lending, insurance—without building banking infrastructure from scratch.

Invisible Banking and Ambient Finance

Banking in 2050 is so embedded it often disappears from view. Through a blend of IoT, AI, and real-time analytics, financial decisions occur contextually:

Autonomous cars pay tolls, maintenance subscriptions, and insurance premiums without user input.

Smart homes budget for utilities, repairs, and upgrades, drawing from tokenized savings.

Wearable devices recommend health insurance adjustments based on biometric readings.

Financial services happen in the background—pre-approved, optimized, and settled through secure protocols based on preferences and behavior.

The Platformization of Finance

The dominance of mega-platforms led to the "platformization" of banking. In this model:

Banks no longer serve as end-user brands.

They offer services through APIs and back-end infrastructure.

Value flows through digital ecosystems—commerce, health, education, and mobility.

Think of finance as plumbing: essential, complex, but largely hidden unless something breaks. Platform providers aggregate various banking services into unified, hyper-personalized experiences.

Examples include:

Retailers offering white-labeled credit.

Healthcare apps bundling finance, insurance, and medical history.

Gaming worlds with their own decentralized economies and financial instruments.

Contextual Finance and Hyper-Personalization

Context is king. Banking services now adapt to:

Location: Dynamic pricing and offers based on geolocation.

Time: Micro-investment opportunities triggered during idle moments.

Emotion: Mood-aware interfaces that delay purchases or suggest financial actions based on emotional state.

Personalization engines pull from vast data pools—social, transactional, and environmental—to customize everything from budgeting interfaces to wealth planning.

AI-driven micro-financial nudges have replaced budgets and financial goals. Users are guided in real-time by nudges, prompts, and automation.

Invisible Lending and Credit at the Edge

Credit scoring is now continuous. Instead of a static credit report, behavioral models update in real time. Loans are extended dynamically:

At the point of need.

Based on intent detection.

With instant underwriting.

For instance, someone browsing education courses may get pre-approved tuition microloans embedded into the enrollment process, complete with dynamic repayment tied to future income streams.

"Credit at the edge" empowers unbanked and underbanked populations who previously lacked formal credit histories.

Invisible Payments

In 2050, payments are largely frictionless:

Biometric authentication is standard.

Digital wallets are device-agnostic.

Transactions occur via gestures, voice, or proximity sensors.

Blockchain-based payments ensure instant cross-border settlements with negligible fees. Multi-currency wallets adapt to foreign exchange rates in real-time.

Businesses now pay vendors automatically based on verified delivery and satisfaction data pulled from IoT devices or drones.

Invisible Compliance and Regulation

Invisible banking doesn't mean unregulated. Instead, compliance is embedded into architecture:

Smart contracts auto-report tax events.

AML/KYC checks happen silently via verified credentials.

Risk triggers flag suspicious behavior before it manifests.

Regulators have adopted "invisible oversight," using digital twins, AI audits, and real-time simulation tools to monitor financial ecosystems without human bottlenecks.

User Experience Reimagined

Interfaces are minimal—or nonexistent. Interfaces adapt.

From screens to voice.

From commands to anticipatory design.

From dashboards to digital concierges.

Banking becomes more like breathing: subconscious, intuitive, and seamlessly integrated into every digital touchpoint.

Challenges of Embedded Finance

Despite the ease, embedded finance raises ethical and systemic challenges:

Over-reliance on automation may reduce financial literacy.

Data monopolies risk concentrating power.

Consumer manipulation through predictive nudging must be balanced with consent.

Designers, regulators, and ethicists continue to debate the line between help and coercion.

Conclusion: When Finance Becomes Background

Embedded and invisible banking represents a paradigm shift—from active management to ambient enablement. In 2050, people rarely "do" banking. They live lives enriched and empowered by financial tools running quietly in the background.

This transformation marks not just a technological evolution but a cultural one. As finance dissolves into the fabric of daily life, the very definition of banking is rewritten.

Invisible to the eye. Integral to the experience.

Chapter 6: Green Finance and Sustainability-Linked Banking

By 2050, banking is no longer neutral in the climate equation. It is a force actively shaping planetary outcomes. Green finance has evolved from a niche concern to a core pillar of the financial system. Environmental, social, and governance (ESG) criteria are now encoded into algorithms, pricing models, and credit policies.

This chapter explores how the future of banking is tightly coupled with the future of the planet—and how finance became one of the most powerful levers in the fight for sustainability.

The Emergence of Climate-Conscious Capital

In the early 2020s, ESG investing surged. By 2050, every major bank, investment firm, and credit agency has embedded sustainability as a primary criterion for decision-making.

Capital flows favor low-carbon projects, regenerative agriculture, circular economy ventures, and green technology. Banks penalize carbon-heavy businesses through higher interest rates, limited credit, or exclusion from services altogether.

Sustainability is not just moral—it's material. Climate risk is now financial risk.

Sustainability-Linked Loans and Bonds

A major innovation is the proliferation of sustainability-linked instruments:

Sustainability-linked loans (SLLs): Companies receive lower interest rates if they meet carbon reduction or diversity targets.

Green bonds: Funding for specific climate-aligned projects.

Transition bonds: For industries in the process of decarbonizing.

Terms are dynamic. Machine learning models adjust loan pricing based on verified emissions data, satellite imagery, and third-party audits.

Failure to meet green targets triggers financial penalties. Success unlocks preferential terms and higher capital access.

Climate Risk in Credit Ratings

Credit scoring models now integrate:

Carbon exposure.

Water usage.

Biodiversity impact.

Supply chain ethics.

These environmental metrics influence everything—from mortgage rates to sovereign bond yields. Cities investing in climate resilience receive better terms. Coastal properties vulnerable to sea-level rise see diminished loan-to-value ratios.

Insurance pricing is similarly climate-aware, with premiums tied to adaptive capacity and real-time risk assessment.

Carbon Accounting and Net-Zero Portfolios

Every financial institution is now subject to stringent carbon accounting standards. Scope 1, 2, and 3 emissions across portfolios are disclosed, audited, and algorithmically analyzed.

Banks and asset managers maintain net-zero portfolios, allocating capital to align with global carbon budgets. AI-powered dashboards simulate the climate impact of investment decisions over time.

Those failing to meet emissions goals face reputational damage, divestment campaigns, and algorithmic downgrades by ESG index providers.

Tokenized Carbon Markets

The rise of blockchain-enabled carbon markets has brought liquidity and transparency to emissions trading.

Carbon credits are tokenized and traded peer-to-peer.

Smart contracts ensure real-time retirement or reissuance.

AI oracles verify impact, eliminating greenwashing.

Corporates, governments, and individuals offset emissions with programmable carbon tokens embedded into products and services.

New financial instruments allow speculation, hedging, and risk transfer in environmental markets, creating deeper alignment between climate goals and capital incentives.

Regenerative Finance and Community-Led Models

Beyond carbon neutrality, regenerative finance (ReFi) supports systems that restore rather than deplete. This includes:

Agroecology bonds.

Decentralized water credits.

Biodiversity-backed lending.

Communities lead local green banks using DAO models, funding clean energy, conservation, and resilience projects. Impact is measured not just in profit but in planetary health.

Crowdfunding platforms connect everyday investors to tree planting, coral reef restoration, and carbon farming—verified through satellite and IoT data.

Climate-Responsive Monetary Policy

Even central banks now wield green tools:

Interest rates are adjusted to penalize high-emission sectors.

Green quantitative easing purchases sustainable assets.

CBDCs include climate-linked logic, such as carbon caps per transaction or embedded climate taxes.

Macroprudential policies include climate stress tests, green capital buffers, and systemic risk models incorporating environmental feedback loops.

Sustainability Scoring and Digital Twins

Every business and individual in 2050 has a Sustainability Score—a dynamic rating based on resource usage, waste, emissions, and ethical practices.

Banks use this score for everything from pricing credit to offering personalized financial advice.

Digital twins of cities, farms, factories, and ecosystems simulate the environmental and financial impact of policies or investment decisions, allowing scenario-based green finance planning.

Challenges and Risks

Despite progress, the green finance revolution faces headwinds:

Greenwashing remains a concern without rigorous, transparent standards.

Carbon markets risk commoditizing nature.

Developing nations face barriers to green capital access.

The transition exposes stranded assets and displaced workers.

Addressing these challenges requires a just transition framework, global cooperation, and resilient, inclusive design.

Conclusion: The Financial System as Ecosystem Steward

By 2050, the banking sector no longer asks if sustainability matters—it acts as a steward of planetary well-being.

Finance is not just responsive to environmental change—it is a driving force in shaping a regenerative, equitable future.

Green finance is no longer a sector. It is the operating system of a civilization in balance with the Earth.

Chapter 7: Central Bank Digital Currencies (CBDCs) and State-Backed Innovation

In the banking future of 2050, Central Bank Digital Currencies (CBDCs) are a foundational component of monetary systems worldwide. These sovereign digital currencies have redefined the role of central banks, democratized access to financial systems, and provided a counterbalance to decentralized cryptocurrencies.

This chapter explores how CBDCs emerged as both innovation tools and instruments of state influence—redefining the very infrastructure of value exchange, governance, and financial inclusion.

The Rise of CBDCs: A Global Movement

By the 2030s, over 100 countries had launched CBDCs. Their evolution accelerated due to

The decline of physical cash.

The explosion of stablecoins and private digital currencies.

The need for real-time, programmable money.

CBDCs became a secure, state-backed alternative that combined the benefits of digital payments with sovereign control.

From retail CBDCs used by individuals to wholesale CBDCs for interbank settlements, these currencies now form the backbone of national and cross-border financial systems.

Features and Design

Modern CBDCs possess key features:

Programmability: Smart contracts embedded in currency.

Offline capabilities: For remote or low-connectivity areas.

Interoperability: Between domestic and global systems.

Anonymity options: Tiered access with privacy-preserving layers.

Instant settlement: Eliminating intermediaries and delays.

AI and quantum-secure protocols ensure security, speed, and adaptability.

Infrastructure and Ecosystem

CBDCs operate on:

Permissioned blockchains.

Hybrid distributed ledger technologies.

Multi-tiered access via central banks, commercial banks, and fintechs.

Wallets are integrated into national ID systems, digital passports, and even biometric interfaces. Smart devices—including wearables and IoT hubs—facilitate instant peer-to-peer transfers and automated payments.

Policy Levers and Monetary Innovation

CBDCs give central banks unprecedented tools:

Programmable monetary policy: time-limited stimulus or conditional universal basic income (UBI).

Real-time taxation: Automated collection at the point of transaction.

Dynamic interest rates: Applied at the wallet level.

Geo-fenced currency: Usable only in certain regions or sectors.

This programmability allows for precision in managing inflation, promoting consumption, and responding to crises.

Cross-Border Settlement and Interoperability

CBDCs resolve long-standing frictions in cross-border payments:

Multi-CBDC bridges link national systems.

Atomic swaps facilitate instant foreign exchange.

Tokenized trade finance reduces time, cost, and fraud.

Emerging alliances—such as the Digital Currency Interoperability Grid (DCIG)—create seamless global liquidity corridors.

Diaspora communities send remittances in real time with minimal fees, boosting financial inclusion and global economic resilience.

Financial Inclusion and Digital Identity

CBDCs empower billions by:

Providing access to digital wallets via basic mobile devices.

Embedding financial services into e-government portals.

Linking payments to digital identity and verified credentials.

Micro-merchants, gig workers, and rural communities benefit from direct access to state-backed financial infrastructure without traditional banks.

Humanitarian aid, disaster relief, and pandemic support are now deployed instantly via CBDCs with transparent tracking.

Surveillance and Control: Ethical Concerns

CBDCs, while efficient, raise concerns over

Surveillance: Transaction-level visibility by governments.

Censorship: Potential to restrict spending.

Loss of anonymity: even with privacy features.

Countries balance these risks by employing zero-knowledge proofs, encryption layers, and decentralized auditing mechanisms. Privacy legislation lags behind technological capability, sparking debate on digital rights.

Coexistence with Cryptocurrencies and Stablecoins

CBDCs coexist with:

Decentralized cryptocurrencies (e.g., Bitcoin, Ethereum).

Private stablecoins issued by corporations or DAOs.

Each serves a distinct role:

CBDCs = legal tender and state monetary policy.

Cryptos = investment, decentralized finance (DeFi).

Stablecoins = programmable payments in private ecosystems.

Regulators enforce interoperability, anti-fraud standards, and synthetic CBDC rules to harmonize the landscape.

The Role of Central Banks in 2050

Central banks are no longer passive monetary guardians. They are:

Tech innovators.

Cyber-resilience hubs.

Architects of programmable economies.

Through CBDCs, they ensure:

National competitiveness.

Financial sovereignty.

Real-time macroeconomic steering.

Conclusion: A New Era of Sovereign Digital Money

By 2050, CBDCs have rewritten the blueprint of national and global finance. They offer the agility of fintech with the trust of state backing.

The success of CBDCs lies not only in technological deployment but in governance—balancing innovation with oversight, inclusion with control, and sovereignty with interoperability.

In the digital age, money is no longer just a medium of exchange. It is a programmable, dynamic tool of economic coordination—and CBDCs are at the heart of this transformation.

Chapter 8: Banking and the Rise of Artificial Intelligence

By 2050, artificial intelligence (AI) is the unseen engine of global finance. It powers every transaction, audit, and decision across banking systems—from fraud detection and credit underwriting to personalized financial advising and dynamic market prediction.

This chapter explores how AI has become a foundational pillar of banking, transforming it into a self-learning, adaptive, and anticipatory ecosystem.

AI as the Financial Nervous System

In modern banking, AI is no longer a support tool—it is the core architecture. Financial institutions operate on:

Neural networks for real-time transaction monitoring.

Natural language processing (NLP) for client interactions and document parsing.

Reinforcement learning for portfolio optimization and risk management.

Computer vision for identity verification and remote onboarding.

Every click, swipe, voice command, and behavior becomes data. AI continuously analyzes these data points to improve efficiency, security, and personalization.

Personalized Banking: AI as Your Financial Twin

By 2050, every individual has an AI-powered financial twin—a digital advisor trained on their:

Spending habits.

Savings goals.

Risk appetite.

Life milestones.

These twins offer:

Hyper-personalized investment strategies.

Real-time budgeting and savings nudges.

AI-driven tax optimization.

Seamless financial planning across platforms.

Clients interact with voice-enabled bots, holographic assistants, or thought-to-command interfaces. Banking becomes ambient—always on, always optimizing.

AI in Risk and Compliance

Regulatory compliance is fully automated using

AI-powered regtech platforms.

Real-time monitoring of transactions for anti-money laundering (AML).

Predictive analytics to detect insider threats or market abuse.

Dynamic rule engines that adjust to shifting regulations across jurisdictions.

Audits are conducted autonomously. Regulatory sandboxes are AI-managed. Compliance becomes proactive rather than reactive.

Algorithmic Lending and Credit Scoring

Creditworthiness is assessed not just by past repayment history but through

Psychometric data.

Social graph analysis.

Behavioral economics indicators.

AI algorithms continuously refine scoring models to reduce bias, expand access, and improve prediction accuracy. Loan decisions are instant, transparent, and context-aware.

Credit becomes a dynamic product—adjusting limits, interest rates, and terms based on real-time financial behavior.

Predictive Banking and Market Intelligence

AI forecasts not only market trends but also customer needs.

Predicts when a client might need a mortgage, insurance, or education loan.

Anticipates life changes (job shift, relocation, retirement).

Detects financial distress early and proposes solutions.

Banks use AI for:

Real-time sentiment analysis across news, social media, and trade flows.

Adaptive trading algorithms in both retail and institutional markets.

Crisis detection using geopolitical, climatic, and economic signals.

Autonomous Finance Operations

Entire financial functions are now run by autonomous systems:

Treasury management.

Currency trading.

Risk modeling.

Client onboarding and KYC.

These systems self-correct, self-update, and self-defend. Human oversight remains, but AI carries out 90% of decisions autonomously.

AI and Ethical Banking

AI's deep integration brings ethical dilemmas:

Bias in models due to flawed training data.

Explainability in high-stakes decisions.

Surveillance vs. privacy.

Job displacement due to automation.

To address this, banks:

Employ AI ethics officers.

Use explainable AI (XAI) for transparency.

Engage in continuous bias audits.

Invest in reskilling human workforces.

AI governance is now a core competency, with boards responsible for algorithmic accountability.

Quantum AI and the Future Frontier

Quantum computing accelerates AI.

Models run at exponential speeds.

Complex simulations become tractable.

Fraud detection and encryption move to quantum-safe algorithms.

Quantum-AI hybrids unlock predictive powers that redefine risk, valuation, and portfolio construction.

Banks also adopt synthetic data generation and generative AI for scenario modeling, client engagement, and even code writing.

Conclusion: Augmented Banking Intelligence

By 2050, AI is the silent partner in every financial transaction. It enables banking that is

Adaptive.

Predictive.

Ethical.

Hyper-personalized.

Yet AI is not a replacement for human values—it is an augmentation of them. The future of banking is not machine-run but machine-enhanced, with trust, transparency, and intelligence at its core.

In this intelligent age, those who master AI not only manage money—they shape the future of finance itself.

Chapter 9: Cybersecurity, Digital Trust, and Risk in 2050 Banking

As banking becomes increasingly digitized, hyper-connected, and decentralized, the security of financial systems in 2050 is paramount. With AI-driven operations, digital currencies, and cloud-native infrastructures, cyber risk is not just an IT issue—it is a core banking concern.

In this chapter, we explore the transformed landscape of cybersecurity in banking and how institutions have evolved from reactive defense to predictive resilience and digital trust architecture.

The Expanding Attack Surface

The future of finance is built on layers of:

Decentralized ledgers and blockchains.

Cloud-native APIs.

IoT-enabled payment devices.

Real-time global transaction systems.

This expansion of interfaces and data flows creates new vulnerabilities, including:

Quantum decryption threats.

AI-generated phishing and deepfake attacks.

Compromised smart contracts.

Supply chain and third-party breaches.

Banks now view every endpoint as a potential threat vector and design systems with zero-trust architectures.

Cybersecurity Infrastructure of 2050

Leading financial institutions operate

Quantum-resistant encryption protocols.

AI-driven threat detection using behavioral analytics.

Federated learning models for collaborative fraud prevention.

Self-healing networks that isolate, neutralize, and recover from attacks autonomously.

Every transaction, API call, and user access is scored in real time for anomaly detection.

Digital Identity and Trust Anchors

Digital trust in banking is built on:

Decentralized identity (DID) systems.

Biometric authentication (voice, gait, retina, neural patterns).

Tokenized credentials stored securely across distributed ledgers.

Customers control their identity through self-sovereign wallets, granting banks permissioned access rather than static credentials.

AI ensures continuous identity validation using context-aware behavior (location, usage patterns, timing). Fraudsters find it nearly impossible to impersonate legitimate users.

Risk Management in a Real-Time World

Banks in 2050 use:

Predictive risk analytics for market, credit, and operational risk.

Cyber risk dashboards with real-time global threat heat maps.

Scenario simulations using digital twins of systems and economies.

Risk management is no longer a static model—it evolves dynamically as threats emerge and morph.

AI models assess not only technical vulnerabilities but also geopolitical risks, misinformation campaigns, and supply chain dependencies.

Regulatory Technology and Compliance Automation

Compliance with cybersecurity standards is enforced via:

Smart contracts that embed regulations into workflows.

Continuous compliance platforms with real-time audits.

Machine-readable laws that update AI systems instantly when rules change.

Cyber audits and data governance are now perpetual processes, not annual events. Regulatory bodies use their own AI engines to supervise and collaborate with banks.

Crisis Response and Cyber Resilience

When attacks occur, banks deploy

Instant recovery protocols using AI-led triage.

Digital kill switches to quarantine systems.

Crisis communication bots that inform clients in real time.

Cross-border cyber alliances to contain systemic threats.

Resilience is designed into every layer—ensuring continuity of operations, data integrity, and client confidence.

Ethics of Digital Surveillance and Data Rights

Cybersecurity raises ethical questions:

How much surveillance is justified in preventing financial crime?

Who owns behavioral data used for anomaly detection?

How transparent should institutions be about breaches?

Banks adopt:

Transparency protocols to inform clients of data usage.

Ethical AI frameworks that limit invasive monitoring.

Decentralized consent models where users set their privacy boundaries.

Digital trust is earned, not assumed.

Cybersecurity Workforce and Human Intelligence

Despite automation, humans play a critical role:

Cyber threat analysts monitor AI outputs.

Ethical hackers stress-test systems.

Red teams simulate adversarial attacks.

The workforce is hybrid: AI-augmented professionals trained in ethics, technology, law, and behavioral science.

Banks partner with universities and cyber defense coalitions to stay ahead of the evolving threat landscape.

Conclusion: Banking on Trust in a Digital Age

In 2050, cybersecurity is no longer about firewalls—it is about systemic resilience, ethical data stewardship, and dynamic defense.

Banks that thrive are those that:

Embed security into design.

Collaborate across borders.

Balance surveillance with sovereignty.

Digital trust is the currency of the new economy, and those who safeguard it become the guardians of financial stability in the 21st century.

Chapter 10: Financial Inclusion and the Last Mile Revolution

By 2050, the vision of universal financial access is within reach. Billions of previously unbanked and underbanked individuals now participate in the global economy, empowered by decentralized technologies, mobile-first platforms, and AI-driven interfaces tailored to local realities.

This chapter explores the transformation in financial inclusion—from physical bank branches to a borderless, device-agnostic digital finance ecosystem.

The Old Divide: Geography, Literacy, and Trust

Historically, financial exclusion was driven by

Geographic inaccessibility to banks.

Lack of formal identification documents.

Low literacy (financial and digital).

Mistrust of institutions.

High transaction costs.

Banks avoided low-income or remote communities due to low profitability and high operating risk.

The New Inclusion Model

By 2050, inclusion is driven by

Decentralized identity systems using biometrics and blockchain.

Offline-compatible mobile banking for rural and remote areas.

Voice-first and AI-powered interfaces in local languages.

Micro-ledgers and nano-loans that function at hyperlocal scales.

Tokenized value systems based on labor, crops, or social credits.

Financial tools are embedded in social apps, e-commerce platforms, and community portals.

The Rise of Community Banks and Digital Cooperatives

Digital cooperatives, DAOs (Decentralized Autonomous Organizations), and community banks manage localized financial ecosystems.

Members pool funds and vote on loans.

Smart contracts enforce repayment and rules.

AI analyzes local data to guide decisions.

These systems build trust, reduce overhead, and enable communities to be financially self-governing.

Education and Literacy: Empowering the Next Billion

AI tutors and immersive content train users in:

Budgeting and saving.

Responsible borrowing.

Risk and insurance.

Long-term investment planning.

Gamified experiences and AR simulations teach financial literacy even to those without formal education.

Digital finance becomes intuitive—accessible through icons, gestures, voice, and translation layers.

Credit Without Collateral

Innovations in alternative credit scoring allow

Reputation-based loans.

AI analysis of transaction patterns.

Social endorsements and community guarantees.

Data from energy usage, phone activity, or work history.

These systems empower gig workers, farmers, and informal laborers who were once invisible to banks.

Gender and Inclusion: Bridging the Access Gap

Digital finance enables women to:

Own bank accounts linked to digital IDs.

Receive direct transfers from governments or employers.

Participate in peer-lending networks.

Access financial advice without judgment.

Cultural barriers erode as technology provides private, secure, and self-paced access to financial services.

Governments and Universal Access Policies

States now implement

Universal digital wallets for every citizen.

Portable benefits like health insurance and pensions.

Smart subsidies delivered directly to phones.

Financial literacy mandates integrated into school systems.

Regulations ensure that inclusion is not just digital—it is dignified, equitable, and empowering.

The Role of Super Apps and Platform Banks

Super apps integrate:

Payments.

Micro-insurance.

Investment services.

Gig work marketplaces.

With AI personalization and embedded finance, users can:

Earn, spend, save, and borrow on a single interface.

Access financial products tailored to their lifestyle.

Move fluidly between services without switching apps.

These platforms often serve as the only "bank" users ever know.

Global Remittances and Diaspora Banking

Cross-border transfers are

Instantaneous via blockchain rails.

Nearly free using stablecoins.

Integrated into national ID-linked wallets.

Diaspora communities create digital family funds, pooled insurance, and remote property investments—fueling economic development back home.

Challenges Ahead

Despite progress, key challenges persist:

Infrastructure gaps (electricity, internet).

Privacy risks in data-heavy systems.

Digital fraud targeting naive users.

Platform monopolies with unchecked influence.

Addressing these requires a balance of

Regulation.

Innovation.

Grassroots empowerment.

Conclusion: Banking for Humanity

By 2050, financial inclusion is not a charity—it is a catalyst for growth, dignity, and resilience.

The last mile is no longer a barrier but the front line of innovation. And in reaching every last person, the banking system of the future doesn't just grow—it evolves to reflect the diversity, creativity, and potential of all humanity.

Chapter 11: Banking in Space and Interplanetary Finance

By 2050, humanity is no longer confined to Earth. With the colonization of the Moon, Mars, and the establishment of orbital habitats, space is the new frontier—not only for science and exploration but also for finance.

Banking has followed humanity beyond the stratosphere, adapting to a zero-gravity economy with its own rules, risks, and revolutionary opportunities. This chapter explores the emergence of space banking, interplanetary financial systems, and how institutions are rewriting the playbook for a multi-planetary civilization.

The Emergence of the Space Economy

The space economy encompasses:

Lunar mining ventures.

Martian colonization projects.

Orbital manufacturing.

Interplanetary tourism.

Satellite-based data services and networks.

As these sectors mature, they require

Capital investment.

Insurance frameworks.

Payment systems.

Trade finance.

Regulatory oversight.

Challenges of Space Banking

Space presents unique financial challenges:

Communication delays between planets (e.g., 3-22 minutes from Earth to Mars).

Jurisdictional uncertainty across interplanetary territories.

Asset transfer latency and consensus protocols in space-based blockchains.

Differing time systems, calendars, and currencies.

Banks must design systems that:

Operate semi-autonomously.

Sync asynchronously with Earth-based networks.

Handle cross-planetary arbitrage and inflation.

Interplanetary Currencies and Digital Protocols

Earth-based currencies are impractical for space. Instead:

Astrocredits and Lunars emerge as local stablecoins.

Smart contracts adjust for time lags.

Interplanetary Reserve Tokens (IRTs) act as a universal medium of exchange.

These are governed by

Space-based DAOs.

Treaty-based monetary alliances.

AI regulators embedded in orbital systems.

Banking Infrastructure in Orbit and Beyond

Banks expand into space by:

Launching banking satellites for real-time ledger access.

Creating quantum mesh networks for secure communication.

Establishing off-world financial hubs with local data centers.

Lunar and Martian branches are not buildings—they are autonomous digital entities with robotic interfaces and AI managers.

Space Insurance and Risk Modeling

New types of financial risk emerge:

Launch failure.

Cosmic radiation damage.

Interplanetary legal disputes.

Psychological factors affecting productivity and decisions.

Insurance products cover:

Equipment and habitat failure.

Life and health risks.

Delays in cargo or crew.

Geopolitical tensions extending into space.

Risk modeling uses:

AI simulations of missions.

Quantum forecasting.

Data from previous expeditions and near-Earth object analytics.

Trade and Credit in the Void

Interplanetary trade involves:

Mining contracts from the Moon or asteroid belt.

Resource swaps between Earth, Mars, and orbitals.

Manufacturing credits for microgravity-produced goods.

Space banks manage

Multi-planetary supply chains.

Floating credit lines for time-delayed payments.

Barter-augmented smart contracts integrating non-currency values.

Legal Frameworks and Governance

International space law evolves to regulate banking through

Interplanetary Banking Accords (IBA).

Space Anti-Money Laundering (SAML) protocols.

Territorial claims and sovereign finance charters.

Banking in space becomes a diplomatic instrument—just as much as a commercial one.

Ethics, Equity, and Access

Key ethical concerns include

Who owns space assets?

Will space banking replicate Earth's inequalities?

How do we ensure inclusive access for all planetary citizens?

New systems aim to

Include space settlers in governance.

Prevent monopolies.

Establish planetary dividends or universal interplanetary income.

Future Visions: From Earthlings to Solarians

Banking in 2050 is not just a planetary affair. It is.

Interstellar in aspiration.

Autonomous in operation.

Equitable in vision.

As humans evolve into a spacefaring species, finance becomes the invisible engine that supports life beyond Earth. The institutions that master this transition will not only shape economies but civilizations.

Conclusion: A Galactic Ledger

The final frontier of banking lies in the stars. Interplanetary finance is not science fiction—it is a natural extension of human expansion.

By 2050, Earth is no longer the only address for financial services. And the ledger that began with clay tablets in Mesopotamia now stretches across orbits, moons, and planets—etched in light, code, and quantum resonance.

Chapter 11: Banking in Space and Interplanetary Finance

By 2050, humanity is no longer confined to Earth. With the colonization of the Moon, Mars, and the establishment of orbital habitats, space is the new frontier—not only for science and exploration but also for finance.

Banking has followed humanity beyond the stratosphere, adapting to a zero-gravity economy with its own rules, risks, and revolutionary opportunities. This chapter explores the emergence of space banking, interplanetary financial systems, and how institutions are rewriting the playbook for a multi-planetary civilization.

The Emergence of the Space Economy

The space economy encompasses:

Lunar mining ventures.

Martian colonization projects.

Orbital manufacturing.

Interplanetary tourism.

Satellite-based data services and networks.

As these sectors mature, they require

Capital investment.

Insurance frameworks.

Payment systems.

Trade finance.

Regulatory oversight.

Challenges of Space Banking

Space presents unique financial challenges:

Communication delays between planets (e.g., 3-22 minutes from Earth to Mars).

Jurisdictional uncertainty across interplanetary territories.

Asset transfer latency and consensus protocols in space-based blockchains.

Differing time systems, calendars, and currencies.

Banks must design systems that:

Operate semi-autonomously.

Sync asynchronously with Earth-based networks.

Handle cross-planetary arbitrage and inflation.

Interplanetary Currencies and Digital Protocols

Earth-based currencies are impractical for space. Instead:

Astrocredits and Lunars emerge as local stablecoins.

Smart contracts adjust for time lags.

Interplanetary Reserve Tokens (IRTs) act as a universal medium of exchange.

These are governed by

Space-based DAOs.

Treaty-based monetary alliances.

AI regulators embedded in orbital systems.

Banking Infrastructure in Orbit and Beyond

Banks expand into space by:

Launching banking satellites for real-time ledger access.

Creating quantum mesh networks for secure communication.

Establishing off-world financial hubs with local data centers.

Lunar and Martian branches are not buildings—they are autonomous digital entities with robotic interfaces and AI managers.

Space Insurance and Risk Modeling

New types of financial risk emerge:

Launch failure.

Cosmic radiation damage.

Interplanetary legal disputes.

Psychological factors affecting productivity and decisions.

Insurance products cover:

Equipment and habitat failure.

Life and health risks.

Delays in cargo or crew.

Geopolitical tensions extending into space.

Risk modeling uses:

AI simulations of missions.

Quantum forecasting.

Data from previous expeditions and near-Earth object analytics.

Trade and Credit in the Void

Interplanetary trade involves:

Mining contracts from the Moon or asteroid belt.

Resource swaps between Earth, Mars, and orbitals.

Manufacturing credits for microgravity-produced goods.

Space banks manage

Multi-planetary supply chains.

Floating credit lines for time-delayed payments.

Barter-augmented smart contracts integrating non-currency values.

Legal Frameworks and Governance

International space law evolves to regulate banking through

Interplanetary Banking Accords (IBA).

Space Anti-Money Laundering (SAML) protocols.

Territorial claims and sovereign finance charters.

Banking in space becomes a diplomatic instrument—just as much as a commercial one.

Ethics, Equity, and Access

Key ethical concerns include

Who owns space assets?

Will space banking replicate Earth's inequalities?

How do we ensure inclusive access for all planetary citizens?

New systems aim to

Include space settlers in governance.

Prevent monopolies.

Establish planetary dividends or universal interplanetary income.

Future Visions: From Earthlings to Solarians

Banking in 2050 is not just a planetary affair. It is.

Interstellar in aspiration.

Autonomous in operation.

Equitable in vision.

As humans evolve into a spacefaring species, finance becomes the invisible engine that supports life beyond Earth. The institutions that master this transition will not only shape economies but civilizations.

Conclusion: A Galactic Ledger

The final frontier of banking lies in the stars. Interplanetary finance is not science fiction—it is a natural extension of human expansion.

By 2050, Earth is no longer the only address for financial services. And the ledger that began with clay tablets in Mesopotamia now stretches across orbits, moons, and planets—etched in light, code, and quantum resonance.

Chapter 12: The Philosophy of Money in a Post-Human World

By 2050, money has evolved far beyond coins, paper, or even digital entries. It has become embedded in behavior, value perception, and machine logic. As artificial intelligence, augmented cognition, and post-human technologies take root, the very meaning of money is up for debate.

This chapter dives into the philosophical and existential transformation of finance in a world where human agency blends with machine intelligence and where value is not just measured but experienced.

From Tool to Mindset: The Cognitive Role of Money

Money began as a medium of exchange, then became a measure of trust, and now—an extension of identity.

Smart wallets adapt to user emotions and context.

Value is perceived through sensory stimuli: AR overlays, biometric feedback, and even emotional resonance.

Personal economies emerge, where each individual has a fluid, evolving valuation of goods and time.

AI and the Automation of Value Judgments

Post-human systems delegate value decisions to machines.

AI curates investments aligned with user beliefs and ethics.

Algorithms conduct micro-trades based on behavioral psychology.

Autonomous agents negotiate, barter, and optimize across digital economies.

As a result:

Value becomes contextual, subjective, and dynamic.

Traditional economic models face obsolescence in favor of real-time, preference-based systems.

The Death of Scarcity?

Advanced fabrication, energy abundance, and synthetic biology challenge the concept of scarcity.

Universal basic manufacturing (UBM) provides goods at near-zero cost.

Post-scarcity economies devalue traditional currency.

Value shifts from ownership to experience, attention, and unique expression.

Banking systems evolve to:

Facilitate access, not accumulation.

Track reputation, contribution, and innovation.

Decentralized Morality and Economic Pluralism

Multiple parallel economies flourish:

One runs on carbon credits.

Another on reputation scores.

A third on symbolic tokens tied to memories or art.

Ethical banking is no longer niche—it is the default. Users subscribe to financial systems whose philosophies match their worldviews. Finance becomes:

A moral choice.

A lifestyle.

A belief system.

Machines as Economic Agents

AI entities:

Possess legal economic identities.

Hold and trade assets.

Invest in causes or technologies.

Collaborate with humans as co-owners and co-creators.

This raises questions:

Can machines own wealth?

Should they be taxed?

Do they have economic rights?

Legal and economic theories stretch to accommodate post-human actors.

Conscious Capital and Sentient Wealth

Money, in 2050, may be

Cognitive: adapting to the user's neural state.

Responsive: changing form or function based on emotional inputs.

Symbolic: holding sentimental or social value.

Assets evolve.

A digital song encoded with emotion becomes more valuable than gold.

A memory token exchanged between friends becomes a lifetime asset.

Wealth becomes less about accumulation and more about meaning.

Rituals of Value: New Forms of Exchange

In a world without cash, transactions feel different:

Eye contact, biometric authentication, or shared experience completes a payment.

Rituals replace receipts.

Gifting becomes a sacred form of currency.

Societies redefine:

What is owed.

What is gifted?

What is beyond transaction?

Toward a Financial Soul

2050's banking institutions resemble

Ethical stewards.

Emotional mediators.

Philosophical networks.

They store not just assets but dreams, digital afterlives, identity cores, and ancestral data.

Finance becomes a sacred duty—intertwined with existential purpose.

Conclusion: Banking Beyond Humanity

In the post-human world, money is no longer just a utility. It is a mirror of our aspirations, fears, values, and evolution.

The banks of 2050 are not vaults—they are temples of intention, bridges between minds, and guardians of meaning.

As we transcend biology, the way we define wealth may be the ultimate reflection of who—or what—we are becoming.

Chapter 13: Building a Resilient Global Financial System

As the financial landscape of 2050 evolves, so too must its resilience. In an age defined by rapid technological advancement, geopolitical volatility, climate disruption, and systemic interdependence, the global financial system must become more adaptive, antifragile, and inclusive.

This chapter explores the design principles, technologies, governance models, and contingency strategies that ensure resilience in global finance.

The Need for Financial Resilience

The 21st century has witnessed:

The 2008 global financial crisis.

Pandemic-induced economic shocks.

Cybersecurity breaches at systemic levels.

Climate-driven disasters affecting entire economies.

These underscore the need for a multi-layered, self-healing financial ecosystem that can:

Absorb shocks.

Recover swiftly.

Adapt in real time.

Distribute risk equitably.

Design Principles of Resilient Finance

Redundancy: Multiple layers of backup systems, networks, and institutional responses.

Modularity: Decentralized components that can operate independently if needed.

Transparency: Open access to critical financial data.

Interoperability: Systems and protocols that communicate across jurisdictions.

Scalability: Adaptive mechanisms that grow with complexity.

Diversity: Inclusion of diverse institutions, voices, and local systems to avoid homogeneity.

Technological Backbone

Key technologies supporting resilience include:

Quantum-proof encryption for unbreakable security.

Real-time AI monitoring of market and systemic health.

Blockchain-based audit trails for integrity and transparency.

Autonomous recovery protocols for interrupted services.

Predictive modeling using quantum and edge computing.

Financial Firewalls and Digital Immunity

New types of safeguards:

Cyber risk reserves are akin to capital buffers.

Autonomous kill switches to isolate infected financial nodes.

AI-driven fraud detection that learns in real time.

Institutions run "fire drills"—simulated crises—to stress-test responses.

Inclusive Resilience: Equity as Strength

Resilience is not just technical—it's social. Financial systems are stronger when:

Marginalized communities are integrated.

Informal economies are recognized.

Microinsurance, microcredit, and grassroots savings networks thrive.

Digital public infrastructure (DPI) ensures universal access to:

Identity.

Payments.

Credit history.

Social security platforms.

Resilience Through Decentralization

2020s-era experiments with DeFi laid the foundation for:

Community-owned banks.

Peer-insured lending pools.

Decentralized clearinghouses that resist monopolistic collapse.

Distributed systems offer:

Local decision-making.

Global connectivity.

Containment of failures.

Climate-Responsive Finance

Financial systems now include:

Disaster-triggered bonds and insurance.

Carbon-adjusted credit scores.

Climate risk indexes baked into portfolio modeling.

Central banks integrate:

Climate stress tests.

Green asset standards.

Planetary boundaries into monetary policy.

International Cooperation and New Bretton Woods

Global coordination is crucial. By 2050, a new Bretton Woods 2.0 framework:

Aligns digital currencies across nations.

Sets baseline rules for AI and finance.

Create a global resilience fund.

Establishes a decentralized IMF-equivalent powered by smart contracts.

Supranational institutions evolve into

Tech-savvy, data-native, AI-moderated entities.

Conflict resolution bodies for digital trade disputes.

Resilience as a Culture

More than tools and protocols, resilience is a mindset:

Agile training for financial professionals.

Ethical foresight and scenario planning.

Resilience indicators embedded in ESG ratings.

Education systems teach financial resilience from childhood, making it part of civic literacy.

Conclusion: Future-Proofing Finance

The financial system of 2050 isn't indestructible—it's adaptive. Its strength lies in:

Redundancy without rigidity.

Complexity with clarity.

Inclusion without exception.

Resilience is no longer optional. It is the defining feature of a financial system that must serve not just economies but societies, ecosystems, and generations yet to come.

yes

Chapter 14: Conclusion—Toward a New Financial Consciousness

As we stand on the threshold of 2050, the story of banking is no longer just a tale of institutions, currencies, and regulations. It is a human—and post-human—narrative about trust, identity, power, technology, and values. Finance is no longer a separate silo; it is the bloodstream of civilization, flowing through every system—biological, digital, and planetary.

A Journey Through Time and Transformation

We began with the bartering of cattle and cowries, evolved through empires and gold standards, embraced central banking and fiat money, and now hurtle through a decentralized, intelligent, programmable financial future.

Along the way, we have

Witnessed crises and recoveries.

Built empires and watched them fall.

Invented technologies that turned scarcity into choice.

Questioned the role of money in meaning and morality.

Key Pillars of the Financial Future

From this journey emerge several enduring truths:

Trust is the ultimate currency — whether built by code, culture, or community.

Inclusion is not charity — it is structural integrity for a global economy.

Resilience is design — not default.

Technology is only as good as the ethics that guide it.

The future of finance is human-centered, even in a machine world.

A Conscious Financial System

In 2050, financial consciousness means

Understanding the broader impact of our choices.

Demanding transparency and sustainability.

Designing systems that protect the vulnerable while empowering the capable.

Embracing pluralism in economic models.

Banks of the future are not just financial engines. They are:

Ethical institutions.

Emotional networks.

Cultural custodians.

Ecosystem balancers.

The Role of the Individual

Every user of the financial system becomes

A node of decision-making.

A steward of value.

A contributor to systemic integrity.

Financial literacy is replaced by financial fluency—a dynamic understanding of how money moves, mutates, and manifests across platforms, dimensions, and ideologies.

The Way Forward

What lies ahead is not a single path but an infinite weave of

Technologies yet to be invented.

Economies yet to emerge.

Values yet to be redefined.

And in that weave, each individual plays a role—not as a passive consumer but as an architect of the future of finance.

Final Reflection

Money was once metal. Then paper. Then data. Now it is meaning.

To build a better world, we must build better systems of value. And to build better systems of value, we must become more conscious stewards of what we value most: life, connection, justice, and possibility.

Finance, reimagined with purpose and vision, becomes not just a system but a soul.

Terrorism and Global Banking: A Symbiotic Strain

Terrorism, in its multifaceted manifestations, poses not only a direct threat to human life and social order but also a complex, persistent challenge to the international financial system. While bombs, bullets, and propaganda are the visible components of terror, the hidden veins that sustain terrorist groups are financial. Money is the lifeblood of terrorism—it fuels recruitment, logistics, weapons, and ideological expansion. And central to this flow of money is the global banking infrastructure. Over the past decades, terrorism has reshaped banking laws, hardened compliance frameworks, and challenged the principles of financial inclusion and neutrality.

One of the earliest signs of this symbiosis emerged during the Afghan-Soviet conflict, where Western and Middle Eastern governments channeled funds through various banks and informal systems to support anti-Soviet mujahideen fighters. These early networks, often funded via charitable fronts and unregulated banking institutions, laid the foundation for later global jihadist financing structures. Banks such as the now-defunct Bank of Credit and Commerce International (BCCI) became infamous for their role in laundering money for a spectrum of clients—from intelligence agencies to terror-linked entities. The scandal surrounding BCCI in the early 1990s exposed the fragility of global banking oversight and the depth of its entanglement with illicit activities.

The 9/11 attacks marked a seismic shift in the financial world's approach to terrorism. Investigations revealed that the perpetrators used ordinary banking channels to transfer money, purchase tickets, and coordinate logistics. This revelation prompted the United States to enact the USA PATRIOT Act, particularly Title III, which targeted money laundering and terrorist financing. This legislation redefined the compliance landscape for banks globally. Institutions were required to strengthen their Know Your Customer (KYC) procedures, submit Suspicious Activity Reports (SARs), and develop robust Anti-Money Laundering (AML) protocols. Correspondent banking relationships were scrutinized, and the concept of "de-risking" gained traction—whereby major banks began cutting ties with smaller, higher-risk counterparts in emerging markets to avoid regulatory exposure.

Notably, the impact was not confined to American soil. Banks across Europe and Asia were soon swept up in a wave of compliance pressure. Deutsche Bank, for instance, came under regulatory scrutiny for weak controls and facilitation of suspicious transactions linked to the Middle East and Russia. Standard Chartered faced fines for violating U.S. sanctions on countries accused of supporting terrorism. In 2012, HSBC was fined a staggering $1.9 billion by U.S. authorities for facilitating money laundering by Mexican cartels and failing to stop the movement of funds potentially linked to terrorist organizations.

In parallel, international bodies like the Financial Action Task Force (FATF) expanded their mandates. FATF began issuing grey and black lists that categorized countries based on the strength of their financial regulations and efforts to combat terror financing. Being listed had significant implications: nations such as Pakistan and Iran found their access to global finance constrained. Pakistani banks like Habib Bank faced enormous pressure, culminating in the forced closure of its New York branch and a $225 million fine in 2017 over accusations of weak AML compliance and potential ties to terror finance.

The rise of informal banking systems such as hawala and hundi posed additional challenges. While often used legitimately by migrants sending remittances, these systems became conduits for moving funds without detection. In regions with underdeveloped banking infrastructure, especially in parts of the Middle East, North Africa, and South Asia, these systems thrived due to their anonymity and speed. This forced regulators to collaborate across jurisdictions and cultures to monitor and regulate traditionally unregulated networks.

The cost of compliance soared. Major banks like JPMorgan Chase began investing over $600 million annually into cybersecurity and compliance technology. RegTech startups proliferated, offering AI-powered solutions to detect suspicious transaction patterns and enhance real-time monitoring. Despite these advances, the global banking community struggled with a paradox: how to tighten controls without excluding vast populations who relied on banking access for survival and development.

Humanitarian impacts became particularly visible in conflict zones. In Somalia, for instance, Barclays and other Western banks severed ties with local remittance firms, fearing regulatory backlash. These firms were essential lifelines for Somali families relying on diaspora remittances. The closure of these banking channels led to unintended consequences: increased reliance on unregulated systems and financial isolation. Aid organizations such as Save the Children and Oxfam also found their accounts frozen or payments delayed due to risk-averse banking policies that flagged any transactions involving sanctioned regions—even if humanitarian in nature.

Terrorism also accelerated the rise of digital threats. As physical banking systems tightened, terrorist organizations began exploring cryptocurrency and cybercrime. ISIS, for example, was found to have used Bitcoin wallets and encrypted platforms to receive donations. The infamous 2016 Bangladesh Bank cyber-heist, in which $81 million was stolen through the SWIFT system, highlighted how state and non-state actors could exploit digital banking for theft and sabotage. Although North Korea was the prime suspect, the implications were global—banks began reevaluating their digital infrastructure, hiring cybersecurity firms, and integrating blockchain for secure audit trails.

Sanctions emerged as a popular geopolitical tool to isolate terror-linked states and entities. The U.S. Treasury's Office of Foreign Assets Control (OFAC) played a pivotal role in listing individuals, companies, and governments suspected of supporting terrorism. Compliance with OFAC lists became non-negotiable for international banks. BNP Paribas was fined $8.9 billion for circumventing sanctions on Sudan, Iran, and Cuba—some of which were tied to terror concerns. Similarly, ING Bank and Commerzbank faced penalties for processing transactions involving sanctioned countries. These incidents demonstrated how banks were now frontline enforcers of foreign policy.

Meanwhile, the pushback from developing countries was palpable. Many criticized the Western-centric financial system for equating entire nations with terrorism due to the actions of fringe groups. FATF grey-listing, for example, could destabilize a country's economy, leading to capital flight and international isolation. Countries like Iran and Venezuela, already reeling under sanctions, began exploring alternative financial systems, including crypto, bartering, and gold-based trade. China's development of the Cross-Border Interbank Payment System (CIPS) and Russia's System for Transfer of Financial Messages (SPFS) were partly motivated by the desire to bypass SWIFT and Western control.

The legal repercussions for banks became more severe. Arab Bank was sued in U.S. courts for allegedly processing payments to Hamas operatives. Though the bank denied wrongdoing, the lawsuit opened a new front—litigants could now sue banks for damages stemming from terror attacks, even if the bank was not directly involved in planning or executing them. This led to a surge in internal audits, policy overhauls, and heightened screening processes, often at the cost of customer convenience and speed.

The Middle Eastern banking sector, too, was not immune. Leaked documents and whistleblower accounts raised concerns about institutions in Qatar, Kuwait, and Saudi Arabia facilitating terror-linked transfers, whether knowingly or through lax oversight. Qatar National Bank (QNB) was embroiled in controversy after a data leak suggested that some of its accounts might be linked to extremist entities. While no formal charges were filed, the reputational damage underscored the fragility of trust in the global banking ecosystem.

Despite the negative associations, terrorism inadvertently drove innovation in financial technology and governance. Banks adopted machine learning algorithms to predict suspicious behavior, built integrated global databases for identity verification, and collaborated with international law enforcement agencies to share intelligence in real time. Blockchain-based projects emerged, promising immutable transaction histories that could revolutionize compliance. Organizations like the Egmont Group, SWIFT, and INTERPOL began working more closely with banks to identify global financial crime patterns.

However, the balance between security and accessibility remains delicate. Excessive regulation and de-risking have created financial black holes—regions and communities cut off from the formal economy. Refugees, informal traders, and charities often find themselves flagged by automated systems simply due to location or transaction volume. Meanwhile, terrorist groups continue to evolve—using prepaid cards, shell companies, online gaming credits, and third-party accounts to circumvent detection.

The future of banking in a terrorism-impacted world will require agility, diplomacy, and technological sophistication. While most large banks now have dedicated counter-terror finance teams and compliance infrastructure, smaller institutions struggle to meet the escalating demands. Global consistency remains elusive—what is acceptable in one jurisdiction may be illegal in another. The fragmentation of norms and uneven enforcement creates loopholes, inadvertently benefiting those determined to exploit the system.

Ultimately, the influence of terrorism on banking has been profound and multifaceted. From multi-billion-dollar fines and technological overhauls to the redesign of global regulatory architecture, terrorism has left an indelible mark on the financial world. Banks are no longer just financial intermediaries—they are guardians of global security, obligated to detect and disrupt the financial footprints of those who seek to cause chaos. But in walking this tightrope, they must also uphold the principles of fairness, access, and due process—lest they become instruments of exclusion and mistrust in a world already scarred by division.

The Negative Influence of Banks on the Global Economy: A 5,000-Word Summary

Banks are fundamental to modern economic systems, facilitating savings, credit, and capital allocation. However, despite their essential role, they have also exerted considerable negative influence on the global economy, often acting in ways that exacerbate inequality, destabilize markets, and prioritize private profits over public interest. From speculative bubbles and financial crises to systemic corruption and political lobbying, banks—particularly large, multinational ones—have often operated in manners antithetical to long-term economic stability and societal welfare.

One of the most striking manifestations of banking's negative impact on the global economy is the recurrence of financial crises, many of which have been either directly caused or severely worsened by irresponsible banking practices. The 2007–2008 global financial crisis is a textbook example. Originating in the United States, this crisis was triggered by a collapse in the subprime mortgage market—loans issued to borrowers with poor credit histories. Banks, particularly investment banks like Lehman Brothers, Bear Stearns, and Goldman Sachs, aggressively pushed complex and opaque financial instruments such as mortgage-backed securities (MBS) and collateralized debt obligations (CDOs). These products were poorly understood, misrated by credit agencies, and heavily leveraged across the global banking system.

The consequences were catastrophic. When the housing bubble burst, the banks' excessive exposure to toxic assets caused massive write-downs, loss of liquidity, and cascading failures. Trillions of dollars were wiped off global markets. Millions lost their jobs, homes, and life savings. Governments around the world, particularly in the U.S. and Europe, were forced to bail out banks using taxpayer money under the argument of "too big to fail." This phrase—meant to justify emergency bailouts—exposed a disturbing truth: banks had grown so large and interconnected that their failure could bring down entire economies. Yet, the people responsible largely avoided legal consequences. Executives received bonuses even as their institutions were collapsing.

This event underscored a key flaw in global banking: moral hazard. When banks know they will be rescued in a crisis, they are incentivized to take greater risks. Bailouts have effectively socialized losses while privatizing profits. The lack of adequate punishment has emboldened banks to continue engaging in high-risk behavior, despite new regulations. While governments introduced post-crisis frameworks like Dodd-Frank in the U.S. and Basel III globally, loopholes remain. Shadow banking systems—financial entities that operate like banks but outside regulatory scrutiny—have grown. Financial engineering has become even more sophisticated, and risk has been pushed into less visible corners of the market.

Beyond crises, banks negatively influence the economy through predatory practices and speculative behavior. Many large banks prioritize short-term profits via speculative trading rather than productive lending. Instead of financing infrastructure, clean energy, or small businesses, they often allocate capital toward derivatives trading, high-frequency algorithms, or stock buybacks. These practices contribute little to real economic growth but inflate asset prices, encourage volatility, and widen inequality. The dominance of speculative finance has transformed banking from a utility for public service into a high-stakes gambling arena.

The role of banks in amplifying economic inequality cannot be overstated. Access to banking services remains deeply unequal across the globe. Even in developed nations, marginalized communities face higher fees, discriminatory lending, and lack of credit access. In developing countries, millions remain unbanked or underbanked, leading to reliance on informal systems and vulnerability to exploitation. Meanwhile, large corporate clients and the ultra-wealthy benefit from preferential treatment, complex tax avoidance strategies, and wealth management services that entrench privilege.

Banks also facilitate tax evasion and illicit financial flows, draining public resources and harming the global South disproportionately. Scandals like the Panama Papers, Paradise Papers, and the FinCEN Files revealed how banks have actively helped clients hide wealth in offshore accounts, shell companies, and secrecy jurisdictions. Global banks such as HSBC, Deutsche Bank, and Standard Chartered have been implicated in moving billions of dollars in suspect funds, often linked to corruption, kleptocracy, drug trafficking, and terrorism. These practices not only undermine the rule of law but also deprive governments of revenue essential for health, education, and infrastructure.

Compounding this is the political influence of banks through lobbying and regulatory capture. Major banks have entrenched themselves within political systems, influencing legislation and policy to favor their interests. In the U.S., the revolving door between Wall Street and Washington has become a symbol of this entanglement. Executives from Goldman Sachs have held top positions in the Treasury Department, shaping financial policy that often benefits large banks. Similar trends exist in the EU, UK, and other major economies. This undermines democracy, weakens oversight, and fosters a two-tiered justice system—one for the elite, another for the public.

Internationally, banking practices have helped entrench neocolonial structures, where developing nations become trapped in cycles of debt, austerity, and dependency. Institutions like the IMF and World Bank, though not traditional commercial banks, work in tandem with private banks to issue loans under conditions that often favor creditors. Structural adjustment programs have historically demanded privatization, deregulation, and cuts to social services, often exacerbating poverty and inequality. Global banks benefit from such arrangements by earning interest, managing sovereign debt, and facilitating capital flows that leave poorer nations vulnerable to capital flight.

Furthermore, the banking industry contributes to environmental degradation by financing industries that are harmful to the planet. Despite public commitments to sustainability, many major banks continue to invest in fossil fuel companies, deforestation, and extractive industries. Reports have shown that after the Paris Agreement in 2015, banks such as JPMorgan Chase, Wells Fargo, and Barclays continued to provide billions in funding to oil and gas expansion. This undermines global climate goals and illustrates the contradiction between public rhetoric and private action.

The concentration of banking power in a handful of institutions poses additional systemic risks. Global banking has become increasingly consolidated. A small number of mega-banks—often dubbed systemically important financial institutions (SIFIs)—control the bulk of financial assets, market liquidity, and interbank networks. This concentration creates a scenario where failure or misconduct by one can send shockwaves through the entire system, as witnessed in the fall of Lehman Brothers. Smaller banks, credit unions, and alternative financial institutions are often unable to compete, reducing diversity, choice, and resilience in the financial ecosystem.

Moreover, the complexity and opacity of modern banking have eroded transparency and accountability. The rise of financial derivatives, off-balance sheet vehicles, and cross-border entities makes it difficult even for regulators to monitor risk accurately. In many cases, internal risk management systems within banks are incentivized to obscure rather than illuminate potential problems. Compliance departments are often under-resourced compared to revenue-generating divisions, leading to blind spots. The Libor scandal, in which banks manipulated a global benchmark interest rate for years, exemplifies how collusion and opacity can flourish in the shadows of complex systems.

The global south continues to bear the brunt of such practices. From the debt crises of the 1980s in Latin America to today's sovereign defaults in Africa, banks have played a central role in enabling reckless lending, followed by harsh collection practices. Private banks provided unsustainable loans to autocratic regimes and corrupt governments, knowing they would later be bailed out by international institutions or public funds. When crises hit, the burden fell on ordinary citizens through austerity and inflation, while banks walked away with profit or protection.

In addition, the de-risking phenomenon—where banks cut ties with regions, industries, or clients deemed high-risk—has had devastating consequences for financial inclusion. Often a reaction to heightened anti-money laundering regulations, de-risking has led to the closure of correspondent banking relationships, particularly in Africa, the Caribbean, and parts of Asia. This isolates entire regions from global trade and finance, undermining development and reinforcing economic marginalization. Instead of targeting illicit finance precisely, banks often apply blanket measures that punish the innocent more than the guilty.

There is also a cultural issue within the banking sector, especially among top-tier institutions, where profit maximization overrides ethical considerations. Aggressive sales cultures have led to major scandals—Wells Fargo's fake accounts scandal is a prime example, where employees opened millions of unauthorized accounts to meet sales quotas. This culture, driven by quarterly earnings reports and shareholder pressure, fosters short-termism and erodes public trust. It turns banking from a profession of stewardship into a game of exploitation.

While digital banking and fintech offer opportunities for democratizing finance, they also open new avenues for abuse. Banks are increasingly investing in or acquiring fintech startups, often to maintain control over innovation. Meanwhile, they leverage user data for profiling, targeted marketing, and algorithmic lending, raising serious privacy and discrimination concerns. Bias in credit algorithms can reinforce systemic inequality, denying access based on zip code, occupation, or behavioral patterns.

Despite all of this, the regulatory responses to banking malfeasance often fall short. Fines, even when in the billions, are frequently absorbed as costs of doing business. Legal settlements rarely involve admission of guilt. In some jurisdictions, criminal charges against bankers are virtually nonexistent. This lack of accountability perpetuates a cycle where violations are repeated with little consequence. Whistleblowers, who risk careers to expose wrongdoing, often face retaliation or are ignored altogether.

In conclusion, while banks remain critical to the functioning of the modern economy, their unchecked power, self-serving behavior, and systemic entanglement have generated profound and enduring harm. From crisis generation and inequality to environmental destruction and democratic erosion, the negative influence of banks on the global economy is vast. The need for deep reform is urgent—not only in terms of regulation but also in redefining the purpose and structure of banking itself. Banks must be reoriented to serve the public interest, support equitable development, and operate within ethical and transparent frameworks. Without such transformation, their role as engines of prosperity will remain overshadowed by their legacy of disruption and exploitation.

some of the most important central bank governors and heads of major financial institutions globally, along with their impact on the global economy:

1. Jerome Powell—*Chair, U.S. Federal Reserve (Fed)*

Country: United States Impact:

- Oversees the most influential central bank globally.

- Played a key role during the COVID-19 pandemic with unprecedented stimulus, slashing interest rates, and launching massive asset purchase programs (QE).

- Currently managing U.S. monetary tightening, affecting global borrowing costs, capital flows, and exchange rates.

- Fed policies under Powell have triggered debates on inflation vs. growth trade-offs, especially in emerging markets affected by Fed rate hikes.

2. Christine Lagarde—*President, European Central Bank (ECB)*

Region: Eurozone (19 EU nations) Impact:

- First woman to head the ECB and former head of the IMF.

- Known for balancing fiscal coordination with monetary policy in the euro area.

- Spearheaded the ECB's climate policy integration and digital euro project.

- Her dovish stances helped stabilize post-pandemic Europe but have been tested by inflation and energy crises due to the Russia-Ukraine war.

3. Andrew Bailey—*Governor, Bank of England (BoE)*

Country: United Kingdom Impact:

- Guided the UK through post-Brexit volatility and COVID-related economic fallout.

- Faced criticism and challenges for inflation control amidst political instability and energy shocks.

- Played a stabilizing role during the UK pension fund liquidity crisis in 2022 through bond purchases to avert systemic collapse.

4. Kazuo Ueda—*Governor, Bank of Japan (BoJ)*

Country: Japan Impact:

- Recently took over from Haruhiko Kuroda, inheriting Japan's ultra-loose monetary policy (negative interest rates, yield curve control).

- Faces pressure to normalize policy amid rising inflation—would affect global bond markets.

- BoJ's actions are closely watched due to Japan's status as the largest holder of U.S. Treasury securities.

5. Yi Gang (former) / Pan Gongsheng (current) – *People's Bank of China (PBoC)*

Country: China Impact:

- PBoC has unique control due to China's hybrid system—the central bank functions closely with government policy.

- Managed financial stability during China's deleveraging efforts, property sector crisis (e.g., Evergrande), and U.S.-China trade tensions.

- Balancing domestic growth with global currency influence (RMB internationalization and digital yuan rollout).

- Key figure in global de-dollarization conversations.

6. Raghuram Rajan (former)—Governor, *Reserve Bank of India (RBI)*

Country: India Impact:

- Highly respected economist and former Chief Economist of the IMF.

- Strengthened India's monetary framework, inflation targeting regime, and banking cleanup.

- Globally recognized for warning about the 2008 financial crisis in advance.

- Advocates for tighter global coordination between developed and emerging markets.

7. Shaktikanta Das—*Governor, Reserve Bank of India (RBI)*

Country: India Impact:

- Took a proactive role during COVID-19 to support India's economy with liquidity measures and rate cuts.

- Oversees India's digital rupee development.

- Balances inflation targeting with support for growth in a rapidly developing economy.

8. Augustin Carstens—*General Manager, Bank for International Settlements (BIS)*

Global Role: Oversees the "bank of central banks. Impact:

- Influences global monetary cooperation and financial regulation standards.

- Advocates for coordinated central bank digital currencies (CBDCs) and global financial stability.

- Critical voice in cross-border fintech regulation and combating crypto-related risks.

9. Kristalina Georgieva—*Managing Director, International Monetary Fund (IMF)*

Global Role: Heads the IMF, lender of last resort for nations Impact:

- Oversees structural adjustment loans and economic surveillance in over 190 member nations.

- Played a central role in pandemic relief and debt restructuring for low-income countries.

- Strong advocate for inclusive growth, climate resilience, and economic reform in fragile states.

10. Ajay Banga—*President, World Bank Group*

Global Role: Heads the world's primary development finance institution. Impact:

- Focuses on poverty reduction, infrastructure development, and sustainability.

- **Initiated reforms to expand World Bank lending capacity to tackle climate change and inequality.**

- **Influences policy in emerging markets through conditional loans and investment guarantees.**

Additional Influential Figures:

- **Mark Carney—former governor of the Bank of England and the Bank of Canada, now U.N. climate envoy—is a global voice on green finance and climate-risk disclosures.**

- **Mario Draghi—former ECB president; credited with saving the euro during the 2012 sovereign debt crisis with his "whatever it takes" pledge.**

- **Janet Yellen—current U.S. Treasury Secretary, former Fed Chair—is influential in both monetary and fiscal coordination.**

- **Axel Weber (former)—Former Bundesbank President, known for pushing austerity and tight money policies in the Eurozone.**

Why These Figures Matter:

- **Interest Rates & Liquidity: Decisions on rates affect global capital markets, investor flows, and inflation.**

- **Currency Value: Central bank policies directly influence exchange rates and trade competitiveness.**

- **Crisis Response: Leaders manage bailouts, stimulus, or austerity during global crises.**

- **Geopolitics: Some central banks (e.g., the Fed, PBoC) impact dollar hegemony or reserve currency dynamics.**

- **Financial Regulation: Set global norms for banks, fintech, digital currencies, and climate risk disclosures.**

- **Digital Innovation: Lead the rollout and oversight of CBDCs and digital finance.**

Futuristic Banking: A Unified Summary

Futuristic banking represents a transformative shift in the global financial landscape, driven by innovations in digital technology, artificial intelligence, blockchain, and evolving consumer expectations. As traditional banks adapt to the rise of decentralized finance (DeFi), digital currencies, and neobanks, they face both unprecedented opportunities and critical challenges in areas such as data privacy, cybersecurity, and regulatory compliance. Futuristic banking represents a transformative shift in the global financial landscape, driven by innovations in digital technology, artificial intelligence, blockchain, and evolving consumer expectations. As traditional banks adapt to the rise of decentralized finance (DeFi), digital currencies, and neobanks, they face both unprecedented opportunities and critical challenges in areas such as data privacy, cybersecurity, and regulatory compliance. Futuristic banking represents a transformative shift in the global financial landscape, driven by innovations in digital technology, artificial intelligence, blockchain, and evolving consumer expectations. As traditional banks adapt to the rise of decentralized finance (DeFi), digital currencies, and neobanks, they face both unprecedented opportunities and critical challenges in areas such as data privacy, cybersecurity, and regulatory compliance. Futuristic banking represents a transformative shift in the global financial landscape, driven by innovations in digital technology, artificial intelligence, blockchain, and evolving consumer expectations. As traditional banks adapt to the rise of decentralized finance (DeFi), digital currencies, and neobanks, they face both unprecedented opportunities and critical challenges in areas such as data privacy, cybersecurity, and regulatory compliance. Futuristic banking represents a transformative shift in the global financial landscape, driven by innovations in digital technology, artificial intelligence, blockchain, and evolving consumer expectations. As traditional banks adapt to the rise of decentralized finance (DeFi), digital currencies, and neobanks, they face both unprecedented opportunities and critical challenges in areas such as data privacy, cybersecurity, and regulatory compliance. Futuristic banking represents a transformative shift in the global financial landscape, driven by innovations in digital technology, artificial intelligence, blockchain, and evolving consumer expectations. As traditional banks adapt to the rise of decentralized finance (DeFi), digital currencies, and neobanks, they face both unprecedented opportunities and critical challenges in areas such as data privacy, cybersecurity, and regulatory compliance. Futuristic banking represents a transformative shift in the global financial landscape, driven by innovations in digital technology, artificial intelligence, blockchain, and evolving consumer expectations. As traditional banks adapt to the rise of decentralized finance (DeFi), digital currencies, and neobanks, they face both unprecedented opportunities and critical challenges in areas such as data privacy, cybersecurity, and regulatory compliance. Futuristic banking represents a transformative shift in the global financial landscape, driven by innovations in digital technology, artificial intelligence, blockchain, and evolving consumer expectations. As traditional banks adapt to the rise of decentralized finance (DeFi), digital currencies, and neobanks, they face both unprecedented opportunities and critical challenges in areas such as data privacy, cybersecurity, and regulatory compliance. Futuristic banking represents a transformative shift in the global financial landscape, driven by innovations in digital technology, artificial intelligence, blockchain, and evolving consumer expectations. As traditional banks adapt to the rise of decentralized finance (DeFi), digital currencies, and neobanks, they face both unprecedented opportunities and critical challenges in areas such as data privacy, cybersecurity, and regulatory compliance. Futuristic banking represents a transformative shift in the global financial landscape, driven by innovations in digital technology, artificial intelligence, blockchain, and evolving consumer expectations. As traditional banks adapt to the rise of decentralized finance (DeFi), digital currencies, and neobanks, they face both unprecedented opportunities and critical challenges in areas such as data privacy, cybersecurity, and regulatory compliance. Futuristic banking represents a transformative shift in the global financial landscape, driven by innovations in digital technology, artificial intelligence, blockchain, and evolving consumer expectations. As traditional banks adapt to the rise of decentralized finance (DeFi), digital currencies, and neobanks, they face both unprecedented opportunities and critical challenges in areas such as data privacy, cybersecurity, and regulatory compliance. Futuristic banking represents a transformative shift in the global financial landscape, driven by innovations in digital technology, artificial intelligence, blockchain, and evolving consumer expectations. As traditional banks adapt to the rise of decentralized finance (DeFi), digital currencies, and neobanks, they face both unprecedented opportunities and critical challenges in areas such as data privacy, cybersecurity, and regulatory compliance. Futuristic banking represents a transformative shift in the global financial landscape, driven by innovations in digital technology, artificial intelligence, blockchain, and evolving consumer expectations. As traditional banks adapt to the rise of decentralized finance (DeFi), digital currencies, and neobanks, they face both unprecedented opportunities and critical challenges in areas such as data privacy, cybersecurity, and regulatory compliance. Futuristic banking represents a transformative shift in the global financial landscape, driven by innovations in digital technology, artificial intelligence, blockchain, and evolving consumer expectations. As traditional banks adapt to the rise of decentralized finance (DeFi), digital currencies, and neobanks, they face both unprecedented opportunities and critical challenges in areas such as data privacy, cybersecurity, and regulatory compliance. Futuristic banking represents a transformative shift in the global financial landscape, driven by innovations in digital technology, artificial intelligence, blockchain, and evolving consumer expectations. As traditional banks adapt to the rise of decentralized finance (DeFi), digital currencies, and neobanks, they face both unprecedented opportunities and critical challenges in areas such as data privacy, cybersecurity, and regulatory compliance. Futuristic banking represents a transformative shift in the global financial landscape, driven by innovations in digital technology, artificial intelligence, blockchain, and evolving consumer expectations. As traditional banks adapt to the rise of decentralized finance (DeFi), digital currencies, and neobanks, they face both unprecedented opportunities and critical challenges in areas such as data privacy, cybersecurity, and regulatory compliance. Futuristic banking represents a transformative shift in the global financial landscape, driven by innovations in digital technology, artificial intelligence, blockchain, and evolving consumer expectations. As traditional banks adapt to the rise of decentralized finance (DeFi), digital currencies, and neobanks, they face both unprecedented opportunities and critical challenges in areas such as data privacy, cybersecurity, and regulatory compliance. Futuristic banking represents a transformative shift in the global financial landscape, driven by innovations in digital technology, artificial intelligence, blockchain, and evolving consumer expectations. As traditional banks adapt to the rise of decentralized finance (DeFi), digital currencies, and neobanks, they face both unprecedented opportunities and critical challenges in areas such as data privacy, cybersecurity, and regulatory compliance. Futuristic banking represents a transformative shift in the global financial landscape, driven by innovations in digital technology, artificial intelligence, blockchain, and evolving consumer expectations. As traditional banks adapt to the rise of decentralized finance (DeFi), digital currencies, and neobanks, they face both unprecedented opportunities and critical challenges in areas such as data privacy, cybersecurity, and regulatory compliance. Futuristic banking represents a transformative shift in the global financial landscape, driven by innovations in digital technology, artificial intelligence, blockchain, and evolving consumer expectations. As traditional banks adapt to the rise of decentralized finance (DeFi), digital currencies, and neobanks, they face both unprecedented opportunities and critical challenges in areas such as data privacy, cybersecurity, and regulatory compliance. Futuristic banking represents a transformative shift in the global financial landscape, driven by innovations in digital technology, artificial intelligence, blockchain, and evolving consumer expectations. As traditional banks adapt to the rise of decentralized finance (DeFi), digital currencies, and neobanks, they face both unprecedented opportunities and critical challenges in areas such as data privacy, cybersecurity, and regulatory compliance. Futuristic banking represents a transformative shift in the global financial landscape, driven by innovations in digital technology, artificial intelligence, blockchain, and evolving consumer expectations. As traditional banks adapt to the rise of decentralized finance (DeFi), digital currencies, and neobanks, they face both unprecedented opportunities and critical challenges in areas such as data privacy, cybersecurity, and regulatory compliance. Futuristic banking represents a transformative shift in the global financial landscape, driven by innovations in digital technology, artificial intelligence, blockchain, and evolving consumer expectations. As traditional banks adapt to the rise of decentralized finance (DeFi), digital currencies, and neobanks, they face both unprecedented opportunities and critical challenges in areas such as data privacy, cybersecurity, and regulatory compliance. Futuristic banking represents a transformative shift in the global financial landscape, driven by innovations in digital technology, artificial intelligence, blockchain, and evolving consumer expectations. As traditional banks adapt to the rise of decentralized finance (DeFi), digital currencies, and neobanks, they face both unprecedented opportunities and critical challenges in areas such as data privacy, cybersecurity, and regulatory compliance. Futuristic banking represents a transformative shift in the global financial landscape, driven by innovations in digital technology, artificial intelligence, blockchain, and evolving consumer expectations. As traditional banks adapt to the rise of decentralized finance (DeFi), digital currencies, and neobanks, they face both unprecedented opportunities and critical challenges in areas such as data privacy, cybersecurity, and regulatory compliance. Futuristic banking represents a transformative shift in the global financial landscape, driven by innovations in digital technology, artificial intelligence, blockchain, and evolving consumer expectations. As traditional banks adapt to the rise of decentralized finance (DeFi), digital currencies, and neobanks, they face both unprecedented opportunities and critical challenges in areas such as data privacy, cybersecurity, and regulatory compliance. Futuristic banking represents a transformative shift in the global financial landscape, driven by innovations in digital technology, artificial intelligence, blockchain, and evolving consumer expectations. As traditional banks adapt to the rise of decentralized finance (DeFi), digital currencies, and neobanks, they face both unprecedented opportunities and critical challenges in areas such as data privacy, cybersecurity, and regulatory compliance. Futuristic banking represents a transformative shift in the global financial landscape, driven by innovations in digital technology, artificial intelligence, blockchain, and evolving consumer expectations. As traditional banks adapt to the rise of decentralized finance (DeFi), digital currencies, and neobanks, they face both unprecedented opportunities and critical challenges in areas such as data privacy, cybersecurity, and regulatory compliance. Futuristic banking represents a transformative shift in the global financial landscape, driven by innovations in digital technology, artificial intelligence, blockchain, and evolving consumer expectations. As traditional banks adapt to the rise of decentralized finance (DeFi), digital currencies, and neobanks, they face both unprecedented opportunities and critical challenges in areas such as data privacy, cybersecurity, and regulatory compliance. Futuristic banking represents a transformative shift in the global financial landscape, driven by innovations in digital technology, artificial intelligence, blockchain, and evolving consumer expectations. As traditional banks adapt to the rise of decentralized finance (DeFi), digital currencies, and neobanks, they face both unprecedented opportunities and critical challenges in areas such as data privacy, cybersecurity, and regulatory compliance. Futuristic banking represents a transformative shift in the global financial landscape, driven by innovations in digital technology, artificial intelligence, blockchain, and evolving consumer expectations. As traditional banks adapt to the rise of decentralized finance (DeFi), digital currencies, and neobanks, they face both unprecedented opportunities and critical challenges in areas such as data privacy, cybersecurity, and regulatory compliance. Futuristic banking represents a transformative shift in the global financial landscape, driven by innovations in digital technology, artificial intelligence, blockchain, and evolving consumer expectations. As traditional banks adapt to the rise of decentralized finance (DeFi), digital currencies, and neobanks, they face both unprecedented opportunities and critical challenges in areas such as data privacy, cybersecurity, and regulatory compliance. Futuristic banking represents a transformative shift in the global financial landscape, driven by innovations in digital technology, artificial intelligence, blockchain, and evolving consumer expectations. As traditional banks adapt to the rise of decentralized finance (DeFi), digital currencies, and neobanks, they face both unprecedented opportunities and critical challenges in areas such as data privacy, cybersecurity, and regulatory compliance. Futuristic banking represents a transformative shift in the global financial landscape, driven by innovations in digital technology, artificial intelligence, blockchain, and evolving consumer expectations. As traditional banks adapt to the rise of decentralized finance (DeFi), digital currencies, and neobanks, they face both unprecedented opportunities and critical challenges in areas such as data privacy, cybersecurity, and regulatory compliance. Futuristic banking represents a transformative shift in the global financial landscape, driven by innovations in digital technology, artificial intelligence, blockchain, and evolving consumer expectations. As traditional banks adapt to the rise of decentralized finance (DeFi), digital currencies, and neobanks, they face both unprecedented opportunities and critical challenges in areas such as data privacy, cybersecurity, and regulatory compliance. Futuristic banking represents a transformative shift in the global financial landscape, driven by innovations in digital technology, artificial intelligence, blockchain, and evolving consumer expectations. As traditional banks adapt to the rise of decentralized finance (DeFi), digital currencies, and neobanks, they face both unprecedented opportunities and critical challenges in areas such as data privacy, cybersecurity, and regulatory compliance. Futuristic banking represents a transformative shift in the global financial landscape, driven by innovations in digital technology, artificial intelligence, blockchain, and evolving consumer expectations. As traditional banks adapt to the rise of decentralized finance (DeFi), digital currencies, and neobanks, they face both unprecedented opportunities and critical challenges in areas such as data privacy, cybersecurity, and regulatory compliance. Futuristic banking represents a transformative shift in the global financial landscape, driven by innovations in digital technology, artificial intelligence, blockchain, and evolving consumer expectations. As traditional banks adapt to the rise of decentralized finance (DeFi), digital currencies, and neobanks, they face both unprecedented opportunities and critical challenges in areas such as data privacy, cybersecurity, and regulatory compliance. Futuristic banking represents a transformative shift in the global financial landscape, driven by innovations in digital technology, artificial intelligence, blockchain, and evolving consumer expectations. As traditional banks adapt to the rise of decentralized finance (DeFi), digital currencies, and neobanks, they face both unprecedented opportunities and critical challenges in areas such as data privacy, cybersecurity, and regulatory compliance. Futuristic banking represents a transformative shift in the global financial landscape, driven by innovations in digital technology, artificial intelligence, blockchain, and evolving consumer expectations. As traditional banks adapt to the rise of decentralized finance (DeFi), digital currencies, and neobanks, they face both unprecedented opportunities and critical challenges in areas such as data privacy, cybersecurity, and regulatory compliance. Futuristic banking represents a transformative shift in the global financial landscape, driven by innovations in digital technology, artificial intelligence, blockchain, and evolving consumer expectations. As traditional banks adapt to the rise of decentralized finance (DeFi), digital currencies, and neobanks, they face both unprecedented opportunities and critical challenges in areas such as data privacy, cybersecurity, and regulatory compliance. Futuristic banking represents a transformative shift in the global financial landscape, driven by innovations in digital technology, artificial intelligence, blockchain, and evolving consumer expectations. As traditional banks adapt to the rise of decentralized finance (DeFi), digital currencies, and neobanks, they face both unprecedented opportunities and critical challenges in areas such as data privacy, cybersecurity, and regulatory compliance. Futuristic banking represents a transformative shift in the global financial landscape, driven by innovations in digital technology, artificial intelligence, blockchain, and evolving consumer expectations. As traditional banks adapt to the rise of decentralized finance (DeFi), digital currencies, and neobanks, they face both unprecedented opportunities and critical challenges in areas such as data privacy, cybersecurity, and regulatory compliance. Futuristic banking represents a transformative shift in the global financial landscape, driven by innovations in digital technology, artificial intelligence, blockchain, and evolving consumer expectations. As traditional banks adapt to the rise of decentralized finance (DeFi), digital currencies, and neobanks, they face both unprecedented opportunities and critical challenges in areas such as data privacy, cybersecurity, and regulatory compliance. Futuristic banking represents a transformative shift in the global financial landscape, driven by innovations in digital technology, artificial intelligence, blockchain, and evolving consumer expectations. As traditional banks adapt to the rise of decentralized finance (DeFi), digital currencies, and neobanks, they face both unprecedented opportunities and critical challenges in areas such as data privacy, cybersecurity, and regulatory compliance. Futuristic banking represents a transformative shift in the global financial landscape, driven by innovations in digital technology, artificial intelligence, blockchain, and evolving consumer expectations. As traditional banks adapt to the rise of decentralized finance (DeFi), digital currencies, and neobanks, they face both unprecedented opportunities and critical challenges in areas such as data privacy, cybersecurity, and regulatory compliance. Futuristic banking represents a transformative shift in the global financial landscape, driven by innovations in digital technology, artificial intelligence, blockchain, and evolving consumer expectations. As traditional banks adapt to the rise of decentralized finance (DeFi), digital currencies, and neobanks, they face both unprecedented opportunities and critical challenges in areas such as data privacy, cybersecurity, and regulatory compliance. Futuristic banking represents a transformative shift in the global financial landscape, driven by innovations in digital technology, artificial intelligence, blockchain, and evolving consumer expectations. As traditional banks adapt to the rise of decentralized finance (DeFi), digital currencies, and neobanks, they face both unprecedented opportunities and critical challenges in areas such as data privacy, cybersecurity, and regulatory compliance. Futuristic banking represents a transformative shift in the global financial landscape, driven by innovations in digital technology, artificial intelligence, blockchain, and evolving consumer expectations. As traditional banks adapt to the rise of decentralized finance (DeFi), digital currencies, and neobanks, they face both unprecedented opportunities and critical challenges in areas such as data privacy, cybersecurity, and regulatory compliance. Futuristic banking represents a transformative shift in the global financial landscape, driven by innovations in digital technology, artificial intelligence, blockchain, and evolving consumer expectations. As traditional banks adapt to the rise of decentralized finance (DeFi), digital currencies, and neobanks, they face both unprecedented opportunities and critical challenges in areas such as data privacy, cybersecurity, and regulatory compliance. Futuristic banking represents a transformative shift in the global financial landscape, driven by innovations in digital technology, artificial intelligence, blockchain, and evolving consumer expectations. As traditional banks adapt to the rise of decentralized finance (DeFi), digital currencies, and neobanks, they face both unprecedented opportunities and critical challenges in areas such as data privacy, cybersecurity, and regulatory compliance. Futuristic banking represents a transformative shift in the global financial landscape, driven by innovations in digital technology, artificial intelligence, blockchain, and evolving consumer expectations. As traditional banks adapt to the rise of decentralized finance (DeFi), digital currencies, and neobanks, they face both unprecedented opportunities and critical challenges in areas such as data privacy, cybersecurity, and regulatory compliance. Futuristic banking represents a transformative shift in the global financial landscape, driven by innovations in digital technology, artificial intelligence, blockchain, and evolving consumer expectations. As traditional banks adapt to the rise of decentralized finance (DeFi), digital currencies, and neobanks, they face both unprecedented opportunities and critical challenges in areas such as data privacy, cybersecurity, and regulatory compliance. Futuristic banking represents a transformative shift in the global financial landscape, driven by innovations in digital technology, artificial intelligence, blockchain, and evolving consumer expectations. As traditional banks adapt to the rise of decentralized finance (DeFi), digital currencies, and neobanks, they face both unprecedented opportunities and critical challenges in areas such as data privacy, cybersecurity, and regulatory compliance. Futuristic banking represents a transformative shift in the global financial landscape, driven by innovations in digital technology, artificial intelligence, blockchain, and evolving consumer expectations. As traditional banks adapt to the rise of decentralized finance (DeFi), digital currencies, and neobanks, they face both unprecedented opportunities and critical challenges in areas such as data privacy, cybersecurity, and regulatory compliance. Futuristic banking represents a transformative shift in the global financial landscape, driven by innovations in digital technology, artificial intelligence, blockchain, and evolving consumer expectations. As traditional banks adapt to the rise of decentralized finance (DeFi), digital currencies, and neobanks, they face both unprecedented opportunities and critical challenges in areas such as data privacy, cybersecurity, and regulatory compliance. Futuristic banking represents a transformative shift in the global financial landscape, driven by innovations in digital technology, artificial intelligence, blockchain, and evolving consumer expectations. As traditional banks adapt to the rise of decentralized finance (DeFi), digital currencies, and neobanks, they face both unprecedented opportunities and critical challenges in areas such as data privacy, cybersecurity, and regulatory compliance. Futuristic banking represents a transformative shift in the global financial landscape, driven by innovations in digital technology, artificial intelligence, blockchain, and evolving consumer expectations. As traditional banks adapt to the rise of decentralized finance (DeFi), digital currencies, and neobanks, they face both unprecedented opportunities and critical challenges in areas such as data privacy, cybersecurity, and regulatory compliance. Futuristic banking represents a transformative shift in the global financial landscape, driven by innovations in digital technology, artificial intelligence, blockchain, and evolving consumer expectations. As traditional banks adapt to the rise of decentralized finance (DeFi), digital currencies, and neobanks, they face both unprecedented opportunities and critical challenges in areas such as data privacy, cybersecurity, and regulatory compliance. Futuristic banking represents a transformative shift in the global financial landscape, driven by innovations in digital technology, artificial intelligence, blockchain, and evolving consumer expectations. As traditional banks adapt to the rise of decentralized finance (DeFi), digital currencies, and neobanks, they face both unprecedented opportunities and critical challenges in areas such as data privacy, cybersecurity, and regulatory compliance. Futuristic banking represents a transformative shift in the global financial landscape, driven by innovations in digital technology, artificial intelligence, blockchain, and evolving consumer expectations. As traditional banks adapt to the rise of decentralized finance (DeFi), digital currencies, and neobanks, they face both unprecedented opportunities and critical challenges in areas such as data privacy, cybersecurity, and regulatory compliance. Futuristic banking represents a transformative shift in the global financial landscape, driven by innovations in digital technology, artificial intelligence, blockchain, and evolving consumer expectations. As traditional banks adapt to the rise of decentralized finance (DeFi), digital currencies, and neobanks, they face both unprecedented opportunities and critical challenges in areas such as data privacy, cybersecurity, and regulatory compliance. Futuristic banking represents a transformative shift in the global financial landscape, driven by innovations in digital technology, artificial intelligence, blockchain, and evolving consumer expectations. As traditional banks adapt to the rise of decentralized finance (DeFi), digital currencies, and neobanks, they face both unprecedented opportunities and critical challenges in areas such as data privacy, cybersecurity, and regulatory compliance. Futuristic banking represents a transformative shift in the global financial landscape, driven by innovations in digital technology, artificial intelligence, blockchain, and evolving consumer expectations. As traditional banks adapt to the rise of decentralized finance (DeFi), digital currencies, and neobanks, they face both unprecedented opportunities and critical challenges in areas such as data privacy, cybersecurity, and regulatory compliance. Futuristic banking represents a transformative shift in the global financial landscape, driven by innovations in digital technology, artificial intelligence, blockchain, and evolving consumer expectations. As traditional banks adapt to the rise of decentralized finance (DeFi), digital currencies, and neobanks, they face both unprecedented opportunities and critical challenges in areas such as data privacy, cybersecurity, and regulatory compliance. Futuristic banking represents a transformative shift in the global financial landscape, driven by innovations in digital technology, artificial intelligence, blockchain, and evolving consumer expectations. As traditional banks adapt to the rise of decentralized finance (DeFi), digital currencies, and neobanks, they face both unprecedented opportunities and critical challenges in areas such as data privacy, cybersecurity, and regulatory compliance. Futuristic banking represents a transformative shift in the global financial landscape, driven by innovations in digital technology, artificial intelligence, blockchain, and evolving consumer expectations. As traditional banks adapt to the rise of decentralized finance (DeFi), digital currencies, and neobanks, they face both unprecedented opportunities and critical challenges in areas such as data privacy, cybersecurity, and regulatory compliance. Futuristic banking represents a transformative shift in the global financial landscape, driven by innovations in digital technology, artificial intelligence, blockchain, and evolving consumer expectations. As traditional banks adapt to the rise of decentralized finance (DeFi), digital currencies, and neobanks, they face both unprecedented opportunities and critical challenges in areas such as data privacy, cybersecurity, and regulatory compliance. Futuristic banking represents a transformative shift in the global financial landscape, driven by innovations in digital technology, artificial intelligence, blockchain, and evolving consumer expectations. As traditional banks adapt to the rise of decentralized finance (DeFi), digital currencies, and neobanks, they face both unprecedented opportunities and critical challenges in areas such as data privacy, cybersecurity, and regulatory compliance. Futuristic banking represents a transformative shift in the global financial landscape, driven by innovations in digital technology, artificial intelligence, blockchain, and evolving consumer expectations. As traditional banks adapt to the rise of decentralized finance (DeFi), digital currencies, and neobanks, they face both unprecedented opportunities and critical challenges in areas such as data privacy, cybersecurity, and regulatory compliance. Futuristic banking represents a transformative shift in the global financial landscape, driven by innovations in digital technology, artificial intelligence, blockchain, and evolving consumer expectations. As traditional banks adapt to the rise of decentralized finance (DeFi), digital currencies, and neobanks, they face both unprecedented opportunities and critical challenges in areas such as data privacy, cybersecurity, and regulatory compliance. Futuristic banking represents a transformative shift in the global financial landscape, driven by innovations in digital technology, artificial intelligence, blockchain, and evolving consumer expectations. As traditional banks adapt to the rise of decentralized finance (DeFi), digital currencies, and neobanks, they face both unprecedented opportunities and critical challenges in areas such as data privacy, cybersecurity, and regulatory compliance. Futuristic banking represents a transformative shift in the global financial landscape, driven by innovations in digital technology, artificial intelligence, blockchain, and evolving consumer expectations. As traditional banks adapt to the rise of decentralized finance (DeFi), digital currencies, and neobanks, they face both unprecedented opportunities and critical challenges in areas such as data privacy, cybersecurity, and regulatory compliance. Futuristic banking represents a transformative shift in the global financial landscape, driven by innovations in digital technology, artificial intelligence, blockchain, and evolving consumer expectations. As traditional banks adapt to the rise of decentralized finance (DeFi), digital currencies, and neobanks, they face both unprecedented opportunities and critical challenges in areas such as data privacy, cybersecurity, and regulatory compliance. Futuristic banking represents a transformative shift in the global financial landscape, driven by innovations in digital technology, artificial intelligence, blockchain, and evolving consumer expectations. As traditional banks adapt to the rise of decentralized finance (DeFi), digital currencies, and neobanks, they face both unprecedented opportunities and critical challenges in areas such as data privacy, cybersecurity, and regulatory compliance. Futuristic banking represents a transformative shift in the global financial landscape, driven by innovations in digital technology, artificial intelligence, blockchain, and evolving consumer expectations. As traditional banks adapt to the rise of decentralized finance (DeFi), digital currencies, and neobanks, they face both unprecedented opportunities and critical challenges in areas such as data privacy, cybersecurity, and regulatory compliance. Futuristic banking represents a transformative shift in the global financial landscape, driven by innovations in digital technology, artificial intelligence, blockchain, and evolving consumer expectations. As traditional banks adapt to the rise of decentralized finance (DeFi), digital currencies, and neobanks, they face both unprecedented opportunities and critical challenges in areas such as data privacy, cybersecurity, and regulatory compliance. Futuristic banking represents a transformative shift in the global financial landscape, driven by innovations in digital technology, artificial intelligence, blockchain, and evolving consumer expectations. As traditional banks adapt to the rise of decentralized finance (DeFi), digital currencies, and neobanks, they face both unprecedented opportunities and critical challenges in areas such as data privacy, cybersecurity, and regulatory compliance. Futuristic banking represents a transformative shift in the global financial landscape, driven by innovations in digital technology, artificial intelligence, blockchain, and evolving consumer expectations. As traditional banks adapt to the rise of decentralized finance (DeFi), digital currencies, and neobanks, they face both unprecedented opportunities and critical challenges in areas such as data privacy, cybersecurity, and regulatory compliance. Futuristic banking represents a transformative shift in the global financial landscape, driven by innovations in digital technology, artificial intelligence, blockchain, and evolving consumer expectations. As traditional banks adapt to the rise of decentralized finance (DeFi), digital currencies, and neobanks, they face both unprecedented opportunities and critical challenges in areas such as data privacy, cybersecurity, and regulatory compliance. Futuristic banking represents a transformative shift in the global financial landscape, driven by innovations in digital technology, artificial intelligence, blockchain, and evolving consumer expectations. As traditional banks adapt to the rise of decentralized finance (DeFi), digital currencies, and neobanks, they face both unprecedented opportunities and critical challenges in areas such as data privacy, cybersecurity, and regulatory compliance. Futuristic banking represents a transformative shift in the global financial landscape, driven by innovations in digital technology, artificial intelligence, blockchain, and evolving consumer expectations. As traditional banks adapt to the rise of decentralized finance (DeFi), digital currencies, and neobanks, they face both unprecedented opportunities and critical challenges in areas such as data privacy, cybersecurity, and regulatory compliance. Futuristic banking represents a transformative shift in the global financial landscape, driven by innovations in digital technology, artificial intelligence, blockchain, and evolving consumer expectations. As traditional banks adapt to the rise of decentralized finance (DeFi), digital currencies, and neobanks, they face both unprecedented opportunities and critical challenges in areas such as data privacy, cybersecurity, and regulatory compliance. Futuristic banking represents a transformative shift in the global financial landscape, driven by innovations in digital technology, artificial intelligence, blockchain, and evolving consumer expectations. As traditional banks adapt to the rise of decentralized finance (DeFi), digital currencies, and neobanks, they face both unprecedented opportunities and critical challenges in areas such as data privacy, cybersecurity, and regulatory compliance. Futuristic banking represents a transformative shift in the global financial landscape, driven by innovations in digital technology, artificial intelligence, blockchain, and evolving consumer expectations. As traditional banks adapt to the rise of decentralized finance (DeFi), digital currencies, and neobanks, they face both unprecedented opportunities and critical challenges in areas such as data privacy, cybersecurity, and regulatory compliance. Futuristic banking represents a transformative shift in the global financial landscape, driven by innovations in digital technology, artificial intelligence, blockchain, and evolving consumer expectations. As traditional banks adapt to the rise of decentralized finance (DeFi), digital currencies, and neobanks, they face both unprecedented opportunities and critical challenges in areas such as data privacy, cybersecurity, and regulatory compliance. Futuristic banking represents a transformative shift in the global financial landscape, driven by innovations in digital technology, artificial intelligence, blockchain, and evolving consumer expectations. As traditional banks adapt to the rise of decentralized finance (DeFi), digital currencies, and neobanks, they face both unprecedented opportunities and critical challenges in areas such as data privacy, cybersecurity, and regulatory compliance. Futuristic banking represents a transformative shift in the global financial landscape, driven by innovations in digital technology, artificial intelligence, blockchain, and evolving consumer expectations. As traditional banks adapt to the rise of decentralized finance (DeFi), digital currencies, and neobanks, they face both unprecedented opportunities and critical challenges in areas such as data privacy, cybersecurity, and regulatory compliance. Futuristic banking represents a transformative shift in the global financial landscape, driven by innovations in digital technology, artificial intelligence, blockchain, and evolving consumer expectations. As traditional banks adapt to the rise of decentralized finance (DeFi), digital currencies, and neobanks, they face both unprecedented opportunities and critical challenges in areas such as data privacy, cybersecurity, and regulatory compliance. Futuristic banking represents a transformative shift in the global financial landscape, driven by innovations in digital technology, artificial intelligence, blockchain, and evolving consumer expectations. As traditional banks adapt to the rise of decentralized finance (DeFi), digital currencies, and neobanks, they face both unprecedented opportunities and critical challenges in areas such as data privacy, cybersecurity, and regulatory compliance. Futuristic banking represents a transformative shift in the global financial landscape, driven by innovations in digital technology, artificial intelligence, blockchain, and evolving consumer expectations. As traditional banks adapt to the rise of decentralized finance (DeFi), digital currencies, and neobanks, they face both unprecedented opportunities and critical challenges in areas such as data privacy, cybersecurity, and regulatory compliance. Futuristic banking represents a transformative shift in the global financial landscape, driven by innovations in digital technology, artificial intelligence, blockchain, and evolving consumer expectations. As traditional banks adapt to the rise of decentralized finance (DeFi), digital currencies, and neobanks, they face both unprecedented opportunities and critical challenges in areas such as data privacy, cybersecurity, and regulatory compliance. Futuristic banking represents a transformative shift in the global financial landscape, driven by innovations in digital technology, artificial intelligence, blockchain, and evolving consumer expectations. As traditional banks adapt to the rise of decentralized finance (DeFi), digital currencies, and neobanks, they face both unprecedented opportunities and critical challenges in areas such as data privacy, cybersecurity, and regulatory compliance. Futuristic banking represents a transformative shift in the global financial landscape, driven by innovations in digital technology, artificial intelligence, blockchain, and evolving consumer expectations. As traditional banks adapt to the rise of decentralized finance (DeFi), digital currencies, and neobanks, they face both unprecedented opportunities and critical challenges in areas such as data privacy, cybersecurity, and regulatory compliance. Futuristic banking represents a transformative shift in the global financial landscape, driven by innovations in digital technology, artificial intelligence, blockchain, and evolving consumer expectations. As traditional banks adapt to the rise of decentralized finance (DeFi), digital currencies, and neobanks, they face both unprecedented opportunities and critical challenges in areas such as data privacy, cybersecurity, and regulatory compliance. Futuristic banking represents a transformative shift in the global financial landscape, driven by innovations in digital technology, artificial intelligence, blockchain, and evolving consumer expectations. As traditional banks adapt to the rise of decentralized finance (DeFi), digital currencies, and neobanks, they face both unprecedented opportunities and critical challenges in areas such as data privacy, cybersecurity, and regulatory compliance. Futuristic banking represents a transformative shift in the global financial landscape, driven by innovations in digital technology, artificial intelligence, blockchain, and evolving consumer expectations. As traditional banks adapt to the rise of decentralized finance (DeFi), digital currencies, and neobanks, they face both unprecedented opportunities and critical challenges in areas such as data privacy, cybersecurity, and regulatory compliance. Futuristic banking represents a transformative shift in the global financial landscape, driven by innovations in digital technology, artificial intelligence, blockchain, and evolving consumer expectations. As traditional banks adapt to the rise of decentralized finance (DeFi), digital currencies, and neobanks, they face both unprecedented opportunities and critical challenges in areas such as data privacy, cybersecurity, and regulatory compliance. Futuristic banking represents a transformative shift in the global financial landscape, driven by innovations in digital technology, artificial intelligence, blockchain, and evolving consumer expectations. As traditional banks adapt to the rise of decentralized finance (DeFi), digital currencies, and neobanks, they face both unprecedented opportunities and critical challenges in areas such as data privacy, cybersecurity, and regulatory compliance. Futuristic banking represents a transformative shift in the global financial landscape, driven by innovations in digital technology, artificial intelligence, blockchain, and evolving consumer expectations. As traditional banks adapt to the rise of decentralized finance (DeFi), digital currencies, and neobanks, they face both unprecedented opportunities and critical challenges in areas such as data privacy, cybersecurity, and regulatory compliance. Futuristic banking represents a transformative shift in the global financial landscape, driven by innovations in digital technology, artificial intelligence, blockchain, and evolving consumer expectations. As traditional banks adapt to the rise of decentralized finance (DeFi), digital currencies, and neobanks, they face both unprecedented opportunities and critical challenges in areas such as data privacy, cybersecurity, and regulatory compliance. Futuristic banking represents a transformative shift in the global financial landscape, driven by innovations in digital technology, artificial intelligence, blockchain, and evolving consumer expectations. As traditional banks adapt to the rise of decentralized finance (DeFi), digital currencies, and neobanks, they face both unprecedented opportunities and critical challenges in areas such as data privacy, cybersecurity, and regulatory compliance. Futuristic banking represents a transformative shift in the global financial landscape, driven by innovations in digital technology, artificial intelligence, blockchain, and evolving consumer expectations. As traditional banks adapt to the rise of decentralized finance (DeFi), digital currencies, and neobanks, they face both unprecedented opportunities and critical challenges in areas such as data privacy, cybersecurity, and regulatory compliance. Futuristic banking represents a transformative shift in the global financial landscape, driven by innovations in digital technology, artificial intelligence, blockchain, and evolving consumer expectations. As traditional banks adapt to the rise of decentralized finance (DeFi), digital currencies, and neobanks, they face both unprecedented opportunities and critical challenges in areas such as data privacy, cybersecurity, and regulatory compliance. Futuristic banking represents a transformative shift in the global financial landscape, driven by innovations in digital technology, artificial intelligence, blockchain, and evolving consumer expectations. As traditional banks adapt to the rise of decentralized finance (DeFi), digital currencies, and neobanks, they face both unprecedented opportunities and critical challenges in areas such as data privacy, cybersecurity, and regulatory compliance. Futuristic banking represents a transformative shift in the global financial landscape, driven by innovations in digital technology, artificial intelligence, blockchain, and evolving consumer expectations. As traditional banks adapt to the rise of decentralized finance (DeFi), digital currencies, and neobanks, they face both unprecedented opportunities and critical challenges in areas such as data privacy, cybersecurity, and regulatory compliance. Futuristic banking represents a transformative shift in the global financial landscape, driven by innovations in digital technology, artificial intelligence, blockchain, and evolving consumer expectations. As traditional banks adapt to the rise of decentralized finance (DeFi), digital currencies, and neobanks, they face both unprecedented opportunities and critical challenges in areas such as data privacy, cybersecurity, and regulatory compliance. Futuristic banking represents a transformative shift in the global financial landscape, driven by innovations in digital technology, artificial intelligence, blockchain, and evolving consumer expectations. As traditional banks adapt to the rise of decentralized finance (DeFi), digital currencies, and neobanks, they face both unprecedented opportunities and critical challenges in areas such as data privacy, cybersecurity, and regulatory compliance. Futuristic banking represents a transformative shift in the global financial landscape, driven by innovations in digital technology, artificial intelligence, blockchain, and evolving consumer expectations. As traditional banks adapt to the rise of decentralized finance (DeFi), digital currencies, and neobanks, they face both unprecedented opportunities and critical challenges in areas such as data privacy, cybersecurity, and regulatory compliance. Futuristic banking represents a transformative shift in the global financial landscape, driven by innovations in digital technology, artificial intelligence, blockchain, and evolving consumer expectations. As traditional banks adapt to the rise of decentralized finance (DeFi), digital currencies, and neobanks, they face both unprecedented opportunities and critical challenges in areas such as data privacy, cybersecurity, and regulatory compliance. Futuristic banking represents a transformative shift in the global financial landscape, driven by innovations in digital technology, artificial intelligence, blockchain, and evolving consumer expectations. As traditional banks adapt to the rise of decentralized finance (DeFi), digital currencies, and neobanks, they face both unprecedented opportunities and critical challenges in areas such as data privacy, cybersecurity, and regulatory compliance. Futuristic banking represents a transformative shift in the global financial landscape, driven by innovations in digital technology, artificial intelligence, blockchain, and evolving consumer expectations. As traditional banks adapt to the rise of decentralized finance (DeFi), digital currencies, and neobanks, they face both unprecedented opportunities and critical challenges in areas such as data privacy, cybersecurity, and regulatory compliance. Futuristic banking represents a transformative shift in the global financial landscape, driven by innovations in digital technology, artificial intelligence, blockchain, and evolving consumer expectations. As traditional banks adapt to the rise of decentralized finance (DeFi), digital currencies, and neobanks, they face both unprecedented opportunities and critical challenges in areas such as data privacy, cybersecurity, and regulatory compliance. Futuristic banking represents a transformative shift in the global financial landscape, driven by innovations in digital technology, artificial intelligence, blockchain, and evolving consumer expectations. As traditional banks adapt to the rise of decentralized finance (DeFi), digital currencies, and neobanks, they face both unprecedented opportunities and critical challenges in areas such as data privacy, cybersecurity, and regulatory compliance. Futuristic banking represents a transformative shift in the global financial landscape, driven by innovations in digital technology, artificial intelligence, blockchain, and evolving consumer expectations. As traditional banks adapt to the rise of decentralized finance (DeFi), digital currencies, and neobanks, they face both unprecedented opportunities and critical challenges in areas such as data privacy, cybersecurity, and regulatory compliance. Futuristic banking represents a transformative shift in the global financial landscape, driven by innovations in digital technology, artificial intelligence, blockchain, and evolving consumer expectations. As traditional banks adapt to the rise of decentralized finance (DeFi), digital currencies, and neobanks, they face both unprecedented opportunities and critical challenges in areas such as data privacy, cybersecurity, and regulatory compliance. Futuristic banking represents a transformative shift in the global financial landscape, driven by innovations in digital technology, artificial intelligence, blockchain, and evolving consumer expectations. As traditional banks adapt to the rise of decentralized finance (DeFi), digital currencies, and neobanks, they face both unprecedented opportunities and critical challenges in areas such as data privacy, cybersecurity, and regulatory compliance. Futuristic banking represents a transformative shift in the global financial landscape, driven by innovations in digital technology, artificial intelligence, blockchain, and evolving consumer expectations. As traditional banks adapt to the rise of decentralized finance (DeFi), digital currencies, and neobanks, they face both unprecedented opportunities and critical challenges in areas such as data privacy, cybersecurity, and regulatory compliance. Futuristic banking represents a transformative shift in the global financial landscape, driven by innovations in digital technology, artificial intelligence, blockchain, and evolving consumer expectations. As traditional banks adapt to the rise of decentralized finance (DeFi), digital currencies, and neobanks, they face both unprecedented opportunities and critical challenges in areas such as data privacy, cybersecurity, and regulatory compliance. Futuristic banking represents a transformative shift in the global financial landscape, driven by innovations in digital technology, artificial intelligence, blockchain, and evolving consumer expectations. As traditional banks adapt to the rise of decentralized finance (DeFi), digital currencies, and neobanks, they face both unprecedented opportunities and critical challenges in areas such as data privacy, cybersecurity, and regulatory compliance. Futuristic banking represents a transformative shift in the global financial landscape, driven by innovations in digital technology, artificial intelligence, blockchain, and evolving consumer expectations. As traditional banks adapt to the rise of decentralized finance (DeFi), digital currencies, and neobanks, they face both unprecedented opportunities and critical challenges in areas such as data privacy, cybersecurity, and regulatory compliance. Futuristic banking represents a transformative shift in the global financial landscape, driven by innovations in digital technology, artificial intelligence, blockchain, and evolving consumer expectations. As traditional banks adapt to the rise of decentralized finance (DeFi), digital currencies, and neobanks, they face both unprecedented opportunities and critical challenges in areas such as data privacy, cybersecurity, and regulatory compliance. Futuristic banking represents a transformative shift in the global financial landscape, driven by innovations in digital technology, artificial intelligence, blockchain, and evolving consumer expectations. As traditional banks adapt to the rise of decentralized finance (DeFi), digital currencies, and neobanks, they face both unprecedented opportunities and critical challenges in areas such as data privacy, cybersecurity, and regulatory compliance. Futuristic banking represents a transformative shift in the global financial landscape, driven by innovations in digital technology, artificial intelligence, blockchain, and evolving consumer expectations. As traditional banks adapt to the rise of decentralized finance (DeFi), digital currencies, and neobanks, they face both unprecedented opportunities and critical challenges in areas such as data privacy, cybersecurity, and regulatory compliance. Futuristic banking represents a transformative shift in the global financial landscape, driven by innovations in digital technology, artificial intelligence, blockchain, and evolving consumer expectations. As traditional banks adapt to the rise of decentralized finance (DeFi), digital currencies, and neobanks, they face both unprecedented opportunities and critical challenges in areas such as data privacy, cybersecurity, and regulatory compliance. Futuristic banking represents a transformative shift in the global financial landscape, driven by innovations in digital technology, artificial intelligence, blockchain, and evolving consumer expectations. As traditional banks adapt to the rise of decentralized finance (DeFi), digital currencies, and neobanks, they face both unprecedented opportunities and critical challenges in areas such as data privacy, cybersecurity, and regulatory compliance. Futuristic banking represents a transformative shift in the global financial landscape, driven by innovations in digital technology, artificial intelligence, blockchain, and evolving consumer expectations. As traditional banks adapt to the rise of decentralized finance (DeFi), digital currencies, and neobanks, they face both unprecedented opportunities and critical challenges in areas such as data privacy, cybersecurity, and regulatory compliance. Futuristic banking represents a transformative shift in the global financial landscape, driven by innovations in digital technology, artificial intelligence, blockchain, and evolving consumer expectations. As traditional banks adapt to the rise of decentralized finance (DeFi), digital currencies, and neobanks, they face both unprecedented opportunities and critical challenges in areas such as data privacy, cybersecurity, and regulatory compliance. Futuristic banking represents a transformative shift in the global financial landscape, driven by innovations in digital technology, artificial intelligence, blockchain, and evolving consumer expectations. As traditional banks adapt to the rise of decentralized finance (DeFi), digital currencies, and neobanks, they face both unprecedented opportunities and critical challenges in areas such as data privacy, cybersecurity, and regulatory compliance. Futuristic banking represents a transformative shift in the global financial landscape, driven by innovations in digital technology, artificial intelligence, blockchain, and evolving consumer expectations. As traditional banks adapt to the rise of decentralized finance (DeFi), digital currencies, and neobanks, they face both unprecedented opportunities and critical challenges in areas such as data privacy, cybersecurity, and regulatory compliance. Futuristic banking represents a transformative shift in the global financial landscape, driven by innovations in digital technology, artificial intelligence, blockchain, and evolving consumer expectations. As traditional banks adapt to the rise of decentralized finance (DeFi), digital currencies, and neobanks, they face both unprecedented opportunities and critical challenges in areas such as data privacy, cybersecurity, and regulatory compliance. Futuristic banking represents a transformative shift in the global financial landscape, driven by innovations in digital technology, artificial intelligence, blockchain, and evolving consumer expectations. As traditional banks adapt to the rise of decentralized finance (DeFi), digital currencies, and neobanks, they face both unprecedented opportunities and critical challenges in areas such as data privacy, cybersecurity, and regulatory compliance. Futuristic banking represents a transformative shift in the global financial landscape, driven by innovations in digital technology, artificial intelligence, blockchain, and evolving consumer expectations. As traditional banks adapt to the rise of decentralized finance (DeFi), digital currencies, and neobanks, they face both unprecedented opportunities and critical challenges in areas such as data privacy, cybersecurity, and regulatory compliance. Futuristic banking represents a transformative shift in the global financial landscape, driven by innovations in digital technology, artificial intelligence, blockchain, and evolving consumer expectations. As traditional banks adapt to the rise of decentralized finance (DeFi), digital currencies, and neobanks, they face both unprecedented opportunities and critical challenges in areas such as data privacy, cybersecurity, and regulatory compliance. Futuristic banking represents a transformative shift in the global financial landscape, driven by innovations in digital technology, artificial intelligence, blockchain, and evolving consumer expectations. As traditional banks adapt to the rise of decentralized finance (DeFi), digital currencies, and neobanks, they face both unprecedented opportunities and critical challenges in areas such as data privacy, cybersecurity, and regulatory compliance. Futuristic banking represents a transformative shift in the global financial landscape, driven by innovations in digital technology, artificial intelligence, blockchain, and evolving consumer expectations. As traditional banks adapt to the rise of decentralized finance (DeFi), digital currencies, and neobanks, they face both unprecedented opportunities and critical challenges in areas such as data privacy, cybersecurity, and regulatory compliance. Futuristic banking represents a transformative shift in the global financial landscape, driven by innovations in digital technology, artificial intelligence, blockchain, and evolving consumer expectations. As traditional banks adapt to the rise of decentralized finance (DeFi), digital currencies, and neobanks, they face both unprecedented opportunities and critical challenges in areas such as data privacy, cybersecurity, and regulatory compliance. Futuristic banking represents a transformative shift in the global financial landscape, driven by innovations in digital technology, artificial intelligence, blockchain, and evolving consumer expectations. As traditional banks adapt to the rise of decentralized finance (DeFi), digital currencies, and neobanks, they face both unprecedented opportunities and critical challenges in areas such as data privacy, cybersecurity, and regulatory compliance. Futuristic banking represents a transformative shift in the global financial landscape, driven by innovations in digital technology, artificial intelligence, blockchain, and evolving consumer expectations. As traditional banks adapt to the rise of decentralized finance (DeFi), digital currencies, and neobanks, they face both unprecedented opportunities and critical challenges in areas such as data privacy, cybersecurity, and regulatory compliance. Futuristic banking represents a transformative shift in the global financial landscape, driven by innovations in digital technology, artificial intelligence, blockchain, and evolving consumer expectations. As traditional banks adapt to the rise of decentralized finance (DeFi), digital currencies, and neobanks, they face both unprecedented opportunities and critical challenges in areas such as data privacy, cybersecurity, and regulatory compliance. Futuristic banking represents a transformative shift in the global financial landscape, driven by innovations.

Futuristic banking represents a transformative shift in the global financial landscape, driven by innovations in digital technology, artificial intelligence, blockchain, and evolving consumer expectations. Futuristic banking represents a transformative shift in the global financial landscape, driven by innovations in

DeFi, digital currencies, and neobanks face both unprecedented opportunities and critical challenges in areas such as data privacy, cybersecurity, and regulatory compliance. Futuristic banking represents a transformative shift in the global financial landscape, driven by innovations in digital technology, artificial intelligence, blockchain, and evolving consumer expectations. As traditional banks adapt to the rise of decentralized finance (DeFi), digital currencies, and neobanks, they face both unprecedented opportunities and critical challenges in areas such as data privacy, cybersecurity, and regulatory compliance. Futuristic banking represents a transformative shift in the global financial landscape, driven by innovations in digital technology, artificial intelligence, blockchain, and evolving consumer expectations. As traditional banks adapt to the rise of decentralized finance (DeFi), digital currencies, and neobanks, they face both unprecedented opportunities and critical challenges in areas such as data privacy, cybersecurity, and regulatory compliance. Futuristic banking represents a transformative shift in the global financial landscape, driven by innovations in digital technology, artificial intelligence, blockchain, and evolving consumer expectations. As traditional banks adapt to the rise of decentralized finance (DeFi), digital currencies, and neobanks, they face both unprecedented opportunities and critical challenges in areas such as data privacy, cybersecurity, and regulatory compliance. Futuristic banking represents a transformative shift in the global financial landscape, driven by innovations in digital technology, artificial intelligence, blockchain, and evolving consumer expectations. As traditional banks adapt to the rise of decentralized finance (DeFi), digital currencies, and neobanks, they face both unprecedented opportunities and critical challenges in areas such as data privacy, cybersecurity, and regulatory compliance. Futuristic banking represents a transformative shift in the global financial landscape, driven by innovations in digital technology, artificial intelligence, blockchain, and evolving consumer expectations. As traditional banks adapt to the rise of decentralized finance (DeFi), digital currencies, and neobanks, they face both unprecedented opportunities and critical challenges in areas such as data privacy, cybersecurity, and regulatory compliance. Futuristic banking represents a transformative shift in the global financial landscape, driven by innovations in digital technology, artificial intelligence, blockchain, and evolving consumer expectations. As traditional banks adapt to the rise of decentralized finance (DeFi), digital currencies, and neobanks, they face both unprecedented opportunities and critical challenges in areas such as data privacy, cybersecurity, and regulatory compliance. Futuristic banking represents a transformative shift in the global financial landscape, driven by innovations in digital technology, artificial intelligence, blockchain, and evolving consumer expectations. As traditional banks adapt to the rise of decentralized finance (DeFi), digital currencies, and neobanks, they face both unprecedented opportunities and critical challenges in areas such as data privacy, cybersecurity, and regulatory compliance. Futuristic banking represents a transformative shift in the global financial landscape, driven by innovations in digital technology, artificial intelligence, blockchain, and evolving consumer expectations. As traditional banks adapt to the rise of decentralized finance (DeFi), digital currencies, and neobanks, they face both unprecedented opportunities and critical challenges in areas such as data privacy, cybersecurity, and regulatory compliance. Futuristic banking represents a transformative shift in the global financial landscape, driven by innovations in digital technology, artificial intelligence, blockchain, and evolving consumer expectations. As traditional banks adapt to the rise of decentralized finance (DeFi), digital currencies, and neobanks, they face both unprecedented opportunities and critical challenges in areas such as data privacy, cybersecurity, and regulatory compliance. Futuristic banking represents a transformative shift in the global financial landscape, driven by innovations in digital technology, artificial intelligence, blockchain, and evolving consumer expectations. As traditional banks adapt to the rise of decentralized finance (DeFi), digital currencies, and neobanks, they face both unprecedented opportunities and critical challenges in areas such as data privacy, cybersecurity, and regulatory compliance. Futuristic banking represents a transformative shift in the global financial landscape, driven by innovations in digital technology, artificial intelligence, blockchain, and evolving consumer expectations. As traditional banks adapt to the rise of decentralized finance (DeFi), digital currencies, and neobanks, they face both unprecedented opportunities and critical challenges in areas such as data privacy, cybersecurity, and regulatory compliance. Futuristic banking represents a transformative shift in the global financial landscape, driven by innovations in digital technology, artificial intelligence, blockchain, and evolving consumer expectations. As traditional banks adapt to the rise of decentralized finance (DeFi), digital currencies, and neobanks, they face both unprecedented opportunities and critical challenges in areas such as data privacy, cybersecurity, and regulatory compliance. Futuristic banking represents a transformative shift in the global financial landscape, driven by innovations in digital technology, artificial intelligence, blockchain, and evolving consumer expectations. As traditional banks adapt to the rise of decentralized finance (DeFi), digital currencies, and neobanks, they face both unprecedented opportunities and critical challenges in areas such as data privacy, cybersecurity, and regulatory compliance. Futuristic banking represents a transformative shift in the global financial landscape, driven by innovations in digital technology, artificial intelligence, blockchain, and evolving consumer expectations. As traditional banks adapt to the rise of decentralized finance (DeFi), digital currencies, and neobanks, they face both unprecedented opportunities and critical challenges in areas such as data privacy, cybersecurity, and regulatory compliance. Futuristic banking represents a transformative shift in the global financial landscape, driven by innovations in digital technology, artificial intelligence, blockchain, and evolving consumer expectations. As traditional banks adapt to the rise of decentralized finance (DeFi), digital currencies, and neobanks, they face both unprecedented opportunities and critical challenges in areas such as data privacy, cybersecurity, and regulatory compliance. Futuristic banking represents a transformative shift in the global financial landscape, driven by innovations in digital technology, artificial intelligence, blockchain, and evolving consumer expectations. As traditional banks adapt to the rise of decentralized finance (DeFi), digital currencies, and neobanks, they face both unprecedented opportunities and critical challenges in areas such as data privacy, cybersecurity, and regulatory compliance. Futuristic banking represents a transformative shift in the global financial landscape, driven by innovations in digital technology, artificial intelligence, blockchain, and evolving consumer expectations. As traditional banks adapt to the rise of decentralized finance (DeFi), digital currencies, and neobanks, they face both unprecedented opportunities and critical challenges in areas such as data privacy, cybersecurity, and regulatory compliance. Futuristic banking represents a transformative shift in the global financial landscape, driven by innovations in digital technology, artificial intelligence, blockchain, and evolving consumer expectations. As traditional banks adapt to the rise of decentralized finance (DeFi), digital currencies, and neobanks, they face both unprecedented opportunities and critical challenges in areas such as data privacy, cybersecurity, and regulatory compliance. Futuristic banking represents a transformative shift in the global financial landscape, driven by innovations in digital technology, artificial intelligence, blockchain, and evolving consumer expectations. As traditional banks adapt to the rise of decentralized finance (DeFi), digital currencies, and neobanks, they face both unprecedented opportunities and critical challenges in areas such as data privacy, cybersecurity, and regulatory compliance. Futuristic banking represents a transformative shift in the global financial landscape, driven by innovations in digital technology, artificial intelligence, blockchain, and evolving consumer expectations. As traditional banks adapt to the rise of decentralized finance (DeFi), digital currencies, and neobanks, they face both unprecedented opportunities and critical challenges in areas such as data privacy, cybersecurity, and regulatory compliance. Futuristic banking represents a transformative shift in the global financial landscape, driven by innovations in digital technology, artificial intelligence, blockchain, and evolving consumer expectations. As traditional banks adapt to the rise of decentralized finance (DeFi), digital currencies, and neobanks, they face both unprecedented opportunities and critical challenges in areas such as data privacy, cybersecurity, and regulatory compliance. Futuristic banking represents a transformative shift in the global financial landscape, driven by innovations in digital technology, artificial intelligence, blockchain, and evolving consumer expectations. As traditional banks adapt to the rise of decentralized finance (DeFi), digital currencies, and neobanks, they face both unprecedented opportunities and critical challenges in areas such as data privacy, cybersecurity, and regulatory compliance. Futuristic banking represents a transformative shift in the global financial landscape, driven by innovations in digital technology, artificial intelligence, blockchain, and evolving consumer expectations. As traditional banks adapt to the rise of decentralized finance (DeFi), digital currencies, and neobanks, they face both unprecedented opportunities and critical challenges in areas such as data privacy, cybersecurity, and regulatory compliance. Futuristic banking represents a transformative shift in the global financial landscape, driven by innovations in digital technology, artificial intelligence, blockchain, and evolving consumer expectations. As traditional banks adapt to the rise of decentralized finance (DeFi), digital currencies, and neobanks, they face both unprecedented opportunities and critical challenges in areas such as data privacy, cybersecurity, and regulatory compliance. Futuristic banking represents a transformative shift in the global financial landscape, driven by innovations in digital technology, artificial intelligence, blockchain, and evolving consumer expectations. As traditional banks adapt to the rise of decentralized finance (DeFi), digital currencies, and neobanks, they face both unprecedented opportunities and critical challenges in areas such as data privacy, cybersecurity, and regulatory compliance. Futuristic banking represents a transformative shift in the global financial landscape, driven by innovations in digital technology, artificial intelligence, blockchain, and evolving consumer expectations. As traditional banks adapt to the rise of decentralized finance (DeFi), digital currencies, and neobanks, they face both unprecedented opportunities and critical challenges in areas such as data privacy, cybersecurity, and regulatory compliance. Futuristic banking represents a transformative shift in the global financial landscape, driven by innovations in digital technology, artificial intelligence, blockchain, and evolving consumer expectations. As traditional banks adapt to the rise of decentralized finance (DeFi), digital currencies, and neobanks, they face both unprecedented opportunities and critical challenges in areas such as data privacy, cybersecurity, and regulatory compliance. Futuristic banking represents a transformative shift in the global financial landscape, driven by innovations in digital technology, artificial intelligence, blockchain, and evolving consumer expectations. As traditional banks adapt to the rise of decentralized finance (DeFi), digital currencies, and neobanks, they face both unprecedented opportunities and critical challenges in areas such as data privacy, cybersecurity, and regulatory compliance. Futuristic banking represents a transformative shift in the global financial landscape, driven by innovations in digital technology, artificial intelligence, blockchain, and evolving consumer expectations. As traditional banks adapt to the rise of decentralized finance (DeFi), digital currencies, and neobanks, they face both unprecedented opportunities and critical challenges in areas such as data privacy, cybersecurity, and regulatory compliance. Futuristic banking represents a transformative shift in the global financial landscape, driven by innovations in digital technology, artificial intelligence, blockchain, and evolving consumer expectations. As traditional banks adapt to the rise of decentralized finance (DeFi), digital currencies, and neobanks, they face both unprecedented opportunities and critical challenges in areas such as data privacy, cybersecurity, and regulatory compliance. Futuristic banking represents a transformative shift in the global financial landscape, driven by innovations in digital technology, artificial intelligence, blockchain, and evolving consumer expectations. As traditional banks adapt to the rise of decentralized finance (DeFi), digital currencies, and neobanks, they face both unprecedented opportunities and critical challenges in areas such as data privacy, cybersecurity, and regulatory compliance. Futuristic banking represents a transformative shift in the global financial landscape, driven by innovations in digital technology, artificial intelligence, blockchain, and evolving consumer expectations. As traditional banks adapt to the rise of decentralized finance (DeFi), digital currencies, and neobanks, they face both unprecedented opportunities and critical challenges in areas such as data privacy, cybersecurity, and regulatory compliance. Futuristic banking represents a transformative shift in the global financial landscape, driven by innovations in digital technology, artificial intelligence, blockchain, and evolving consumer expectations. As traditional banks adapt to the rise of decentralized finance (DeFi), digital currencies, and neobanks, they face both unprecedented opportunities and critical challenges in areas such as data privacy, cybersecurity, and regulatory compliance. Futuristic banking represents a transformative shift in the global financial landscape, driven by innovations in digital technology, artificial intelligence, blockchain, and evolving consumer expectations. As traditional banks adapt to the rise of decentralized finance (DeFi), digital currencies, and neobanks, they face both unprecedented opportunities and critical challenges in areas such as data privacy, cybersecurity, and regulatory compliance. Futuristic banking represents a transformative shift in the global financial landscape, driven by innovations in digital technology, artificial intelligence, blockchain, and evolving consumer expectations. As traditional banks adapt to the rise of decentralized finance (DeFi), digital currencies, and neobanks, they face both unprecedented opportunities and critical challenges in areas such as data privacy, cybersecurity, and regulatory compliance. Futuristic banking represents a transformative shift in the global financial landscape, driven by innovations in digital technology, artificial intelligence, blockchain, and evolving consumer expectations. As traditional banks adapt to the rise of decentralized finance (DeFi), digital currencies, and neobanks, they face both unprecedented opportunities and critical challenges in areas such as data privacy, cybersecurity, and regulatory compliance. Futuristic banking represents a transformative shift in the global financial landscape, driven by innovations in digital technology, artificial intelligence, blockchain, and evolving consumer expectations. As traditional banks adapt to the rise of decentralized finance (DeFi), digital currencies, and neobanks, they face both unprecedented opportunities and critical challenges in areas such as data privacy, cybersecurity, and regulatory compliance. Futuristic banking represents a transformative shift in the global financial landscape, driven by innovations in digital technology, artificial intelligence, blockchain, and evolving consumer expectations. As traditional banks adapt to the rise of decentralized finance (DeFi), digital currencies, and neobanks, they face both unprecedented opportunities and critical challenges in areas such as data privacy, cybersecurity, and regulatory compliance. Futuristic banking represents a transformative shift in the global financial landscape, driven by innovations in digital technology, artificial intelligence, blockchain, and evolving consumer expectations. As traditional banks adapt to the rise of decentralized finance (DeFi), digital currencies, and neobanks, they face both unprecedented opportunities and critical challenges in areas such as data privacy, cybersecurity, and regulatory compliance. Futuristic banking represents a transformative shift in the global financial landscape, driven by innovations in digital technology, artificial intelligence, blockchain, and evolving consumer expectations. As traditional banks adapt to the rise of decentralized finance (DeFi), digital currencies, and neobanks, they face both unprecedented opportunities and critical challenges in areas such as data privacy, cybersecurity, and regulatory compliance. Futuristic banking represents a transformative shift in the global financial landscape, driven by innovations in digital technology, artificial intelligence, blockchain, and evolving consumer expectations. As traditional banks adapt to the rise of decentralized finance (DeFi), digital currencies, and neobanks, they face both unprecedented opportunities and critical challenges in areas such as data privacy, cybersecurity, and regulatory compliance. Futuristic banking represents a transformative shift in the global financial landscape, driven by innovations in digital technology, artificial intelligence, blockchain, and evolving consumer expectations. As traditional banks adapt to the rise of decentralized finance (DeFi), digital currencies, and neobanks, they face both unprecedented opportunities and critical challenges in areas such as data privacy, cybersecurity, and regulatory compliance. Futuristic banking represents a transformative shift in the global financial landscape, driven by innovations in digital technology, artificial intelligence, blockchain, and evolving consumer expectations. As traditional banks adapt to the rise of decentralized finance (DeFi), digital currencies, and neobanks, they face both unprecedented opportunities and critical challenges in areas such as data privacy, cybersecurity, and regulatory compliance. Futuristic banking represents a transformative shift in the global financial landscape, driven by innovations in digital technology, artificial intelligence, blockchain, and evolving consumer expectations. As traditional banks adapt to the rise of decentralized finance (DeFi), digital currencies, and neobanks, they face both unprecedented opportunities and critical challenges in areas such as data privacy, cybersecurity, and regulatory compliance. Futuristic banking represents a transformative shift in the global financial landscape, driven by innovations in digital technology, artificial intelligence, blockchain, and evolving consumer expectations. As traditional banks adapt to the rise of decentralized finance (DeFi), digital currencies, and neobanks, they face both unprecedented opportunities and critical challenges in areas such as data privacy, cybersecurity, and regulatory compliance. Futuristic banking represents a transformative shift in the global financial landscape, driven by innovations in digital technology, artificial intelligence, blockchain, and evolving consumer expectations. As traditional banks adapt to the rise of decentralized finance (DeFi), digital currencies, and neobanks, they face both unprecedented opportunities and critical challenges in areas such as data privacy, cybersecurity, and regulatory compliance. Futuristic banking represents a transformative shift in the global financial landscape, driven by innovations in digital technology, artificial intelligence, blockchain, and evolving consumer expectations. As traditional banks adapt to the rise of decentralized finance (DeFi), digital currencies, and neobanks, they face both unprecedented opportunities and critical challenges in areas such as data privacy, cybersecurity, and regulatory compliance. Futuristic banking represents a transformative shift in the global financial landscape, driven by innovations in digital technology, artificial intelligence, blockchain, and evolving consumer expectations. As traditional banks adapt to the rise of decentralized finance (DeFi), digital currencies, and neobanks, they face both unprecedented opportunities and critical challenges in areas such as data privacy, cybersecurity, and regulatory compliance. Futuristic banking represents a transformative shift in the global financial landscape, driven by innovations in digital technology, artificial intelligence, blockchain, and evolving consumer expectations. As traditional banks adapt to the rise of decentralized finance (DeFi), digital currencies, and neobanks, they face both unprecedented opportunities and critical challenges in areas such as data privacy, cybersecurity, and regulatory compliance. Futuristic banking represents a transformative shift in the global financial landscape, driven by innovations in digital technology, artificial intelligence, blockchain, and evolving consumer expectations. As traditional banks adapt to the rise of decentralized finance (DeFi), digital currencies, and neobanks, they face both unprecedented opportunities and critical challenges in areas such as data privacy, cybersecurity, and regulatory compliance. Futuristic banking represents a transformative shift in the global financial landscape, driven by innovations in digital technology, artificial intelligence, blockchain, and evolving consumer expectations. As traditional banks adapt to the rise of decentralized finance (DeFi), digital currencies, and neobanks, they face both unprecedented opportunities and critical challenges in areas such as data privacy, cybersecurity, and regulatory compliance. Futuristic banking represents a transformative shift in the global financial landscape, driven by innovations in digital technology, artificial intelligence, blockchain, and evolving consumer expectations. As traditional banks adapt to the rise of decentralized finance (DeFi), digital currencies, and neobanks, they face both unprecedented opportunities and critical challenges in areas such as data privacy, cybersecurity, and regulatory compliance. Futuristic banking represents a transformative shift in the global financial landscape, driven by innovations in digital technology, artificial intelligence, blockchain, and evolving consumer expectations. As traditional banks adapt to the rise of decentralized finance (DeFi), digital currencies, and neobanks, they face both unprecedented opportunities and critical challenges in areas such as data privacy, cybersecurity, and regulatory compliance. Futuristic banking represents a transformative shift in the global financial landscape, driven by innovations in digital technology, artificial intelligence, blockchain, and evolving consumer expectations. As traditional banks adapt to the rise of decentralized finance (DeFi), digital currencies, and neobanks, they face both unprecedented opportunities and critical challenges in areas such as data privacy, cybersecurity, and regulatory compliance. Futuristic banking represents a transformative shift in the global financial landscape, driven by innovations in digital technology, artificial intelligence, blockchain, and evolving consumer expectations. As traditional banks adapt to the rise of decentralized finance (DeFi), digital currencies, and neobanks, they face both unprecedented opportunities and critical challenges in areas such as data privacy, cybersecurity, and regulatory compliance. Futuristic banking represents a transformative shift in the global financial landscape, driven by innovations in digital technology, artificial intelligence, blockchain, and evolving consumer expectations. As traditional banks adapt to the rise of decentralized finance (DeFi), digital currencies, and neobanks, they face both unprecedented opportunities and critical challenges in areas such as data privacy, cybersecurity, and regulatory compliance. Futuristic banking represents a transformative shift in the global financial landscape, driven by innovations in digital technology, artificial intelligence, blockchain, and evolving consumer expectations. As traditional banks adapt to the rise of decentralized finance (DeFi), digital currencies, and neobanks, they face both unprecedented opportunities and critical challenges in areas such as data privacy, cybersecurity, and regulatory compliance. Futuristic banking represents a transformative shift in the global financial landscape, driven by innovations in digital technology, artificial intelligence, blockchain, and evolving consumer expectations. As traditional banks adapt to the rise of decentralized finance (DeFi), digital currencies, and neobanks, they face both unprecedented opportunities and critical challenges in areas such as data privacy, cybersecurity, and regulatory compliance. Futuristic banking represents a transformative shift in the global financial landscape, driven by innovations in digital technology, artificial intelligence, blockchain, and evolving consumer expectations. As traditional banks adapt to the rise of decentralized finance (DeFi), digital currencies, and neobanks, they face both unprecedented opportunities and critical challenges in areas such as data privacy, cybersecurity, and regulatory compliance. Futuristic banking represents a transformative shift in the global financial landscape, driven by innovations in digital technology, artificial intelligence, blockchain, and evolving consumer expectations. As traditional banks adapt to the rise of decentralized finance (DeFi), digital currencies, and neobanks, they face both unprecedented opportunities and critical challenges in areas such as data privacy, cybersecurity, and regulatory compliance. Futuristic banking represents a transformative shift in the global financial landscape, driven by innovations in digital technology, artificial intelligence, blockchain, and evolving consumer expectations. As traditional banks adapt to the rise of decentralized finance (DeFi), digital currencies, and neobanks, they face both unprecedented opportunities and critical challenges in areas such as data privacy, cybersecurity, and regulatory compliance. Futuristic banking represents a transformative shift in the global financial landscape, driven by innovations in digital technology, artificial intelligence, blockchain, and evolving consumer expectations. As traditional banks adapt to the rise of decentralized finance (DeFi), digital currencies, and neobanks, they face both unprecedented opportunities and critical challenges in areas such as data privacy, cybersecurity, and regulatory compliance. Futuristic banking represents a transformative shift in the global financial landscape, driven by innovations in digital technology, artificial intelligence, blockchain, and evolving consumer expectations. As traditional banks adapt to the rise of decentralized finance (DeFi), digital currencies, and neobanks, they face both unprecedented opportunities and critical challenges in areas such as data privacy, cybersecurity, and regulatory compliance. Futuristic banking represents a transformative shift in the global financial landscape, driven by innovations in digital technology, artificial intelligence, blockchain, and evolving consumer expectations. As traditional banks adapt to the rise of decentralized finance (DeFi), digital currencies, and neobanks, they face both unprecedented opportunities and critical challenges in areas such as data privacy, cybersecurity, and regulatory compliance. Futuristic banking represents a transformative shift in the global financial landscape, driven by innovations in digital technology, artificial intelligence, blockchain, and evolving consumer expectations. As traditional banks adapt to the rise of decentralized finance (DeFi), digital currencies, and neobanks, they face both unprecedented opportunities and critical challenges in areas such as data privacy, cybersecurity, and regulatory compliance. Futuristic banking represents a transformative shift in the global financial landscape, driven by innovations in digital technology, artificial intelligence, blockchain, and evolving consumer expectations. As traditional banks adapt to the rise of decentralized finance (DeFi), digital currencies, and neobanks, they face both unprecedented opportunities and critical challenges in areas such as data privacy, cybersecurity, and regulatory compliance. Futuristic banking represents a transformative shift in the global financial landscape, driven by innovations in digital technology, artificial intelligence, blockchain, and evolving consumer expectations. As traditional banks adapt to the rise of decentralized finance (DeFi), digital currencies, and neobanks, they face both unprecedented opportunities and critical challenges in areas such as data privacy, cybersecurity, and regulatory compliance. Futuristic banking represents a transformative shift in the global financial landscape, driven by innovations in digital technology, artificial intelligence, blockchain, and evolving consumer expectations. As traditional banks adapt to the rise of decentralized finance (DeFi), digital currencies, and neobanks, they face both unprecedented opportunities and critical challenges in areas such as data privacy, cybersecurity, and regulatory compliance. Futuristic banking represents a transformative shift in the global financial landscape, driven by innovations in digital technology, artificial intelligence, blockchain, and evolving consumer expectations. As traditional banks adapt to the rise of decentralized finance (DeFi), digital currencies, and neobanks, they face both unprecedented opportunities and critical challenges in areas such as data privacy, cybersecurity, and regulatory compliance. Futuristic banking represents a transformative shift in the global financial landscape, driven by innovations in digital technology, artificial intelligence, blockchain, and evolving consumer expectations. As traditional banks adapt to the rise of decentralized finance (DeFi), digital currencies, and neobanks, they face both unprecedented opportunities and critical challenges in areas such as data privacy, cybersecurity, and regulatory compliance. Futuristic banking represents a transformative shift in the global financial landscape, driven by innovations in digital technology, artificial intelligence, blockchain, and evolving consumer expectations. As traditional banks adapt to the rise of decentralized finance (DeFi), digital currencies, and neobanks, they face both unprecedented opportunities and critical challenges in areas such as data privacy, cybersecurity, and regulatory compliance. Futuristic banking represents a transformative shift in the global financial landscape, driven by innovations in digital technology, artificial intelligence, blockchain, and evolving consumer expectations. As traditional banks adapt to the rise of decentralized finance (DeFi), digital currencies, and neobanks, they face both unprecedented opportunities and critical challenges in areas such as data privacy, cybersecurity, and regulatory compliance. Futuristic banking represents a transformative shift in the global financial landscape, driven by innovations in digital technology, artificial intelligence, blockchain, and evolving consumer expectations. As traditional banks adapt to the rise of decentralized finance (DeFi), digital currencies, and neobanks, they face both unprecedented opportunities and critical challenges in areas such as data privacy, cybersecurity, and regulatory compliance. Futuristic banking represents a transformative shift in the global financial landscape, driven by innovations in digital technology, artificial intelligence, blockchain, and evolving consumer expectations. As traditional banks adapt to the rise of decentralized finance (DeFi), digital currencies, and neobanks, they face both unprecedented opportunities and critical challenges in areas such as data privacy, cybersecurity, and regulatory compliance. Futuristic banking represents a transformative shift in the global financial landscape, driven by innovations in digital technology, artificial intelligence, blockchain, and evolving consumer expectations. As traditional banks adapt to the rise of decentralized finance (DeFi), digital currencies, and neobanks, they face both unprecedented opportunities and critical challenges in areas such as data privacy, cybersecurity, and regulatory compliance. Futuristic banking represents a transformative shift in the global financial landscape, driven by innovations in digital technology, artificial intelligence, blockchain, and evolving consumer expectations. As traditional banks adapt to the rise of decentralized finance (DeFi), digital currencies, and neobanks, they face both unprecedented opportunities and critical challenges in areas such as data privacy, cybersecurity, and regulatory compliance. Futuristic banking represents a transformative shift in the global financial landscape, driven by innovations in digital technology, artificial intelligence, blockchain, and evolving consumer expectations. As traditional banks adapt to the rise of decentralized finance (DeFi), digital currencies, and neobanks, they face both unprecedented opportunities and critical challenges in areas such as data privacy, cybersecurity, and regulatory compliance. Futuristic banking represents a transformative shift in the global financial landscape, driven by innovations in digital technology, artificial intelligence, blockchain, and evolving consumer expectations. As traditional banks adapt to the rise of decentralized finance (DeFi), digital currencies, and neobanks, they face both unprecedented opportunities and critical challenges in areas such as data privacy, cybersecurity, and regulatory compliance. Futuristic banking represents a transformative shift in the global financial landscape, driven by innovations in digital technology, artificial intelligence, blockchain, and evolving consumer expectations. As traditional banks adapt to the rise of decentralized finance (DeFi), digital currencies, and neobanks, they face both unprecedented opportunities and critical challenges in areas such as data privacy, cybersecurity, and regulatory compliance. Futuristic banking represents a transformative shift in the global financial landscape, driven by innovations in digital technology, artificial intelligence, blockchain, and evolving consumer expectations. As traditional banks adapt to the rise of decentralized finance (DeFi), digital currencies, and neobanks, they face both unprecedented opportunities and critical challenges in areas such as data privacy, cybersecurity, and regulatory compliance. Futuristic banking represents a transformative shift in the global financial landscape, driven by innovations in digital technology, artificial intelligence, blockchain, and evolving consumer expectations. As traditional banks adapt to the rise of decentralized finance (DeFi), digital currencies, and neobanks, they face both unprecedented opportunities and critical challenges in areas such as data privacy, cybersecurity, and regulatory compliance. Futuristic banking represents a transformative shift in the global financial landscape, driven by innovations in digital technology, artificial intelligence, blockchain, and evolving consumer expectations. As traditional banks adapt to the rise of decentralized finance (DeFi), digital currencies, and neobanks, they face both unprecedented opportunities and critical challenges in areas such as data privacy, cybersecurity, and regulatory compliance. Futuristic banking represents a transformative shift in the global financial landscape, driven by innovations in digital technology, artificial intelligence, blockchain, and evolving consumer expectations. As traditional banks adapt to the rise of decentralized finance (DeFi), digital currencies, and neobanks, they face both unprecedented opportunities and critical challenges in areas such as data privacy, cybersecurity, and regulatory compliance. Futuristic banking represents a transformative shift in the global financial landscape, driven by innovations in digital technology, artificial intelligence, blockchain, and evolving consumer expectations. As traditional banks adapt to the rise of decentralized finance (DeFi), digital currencies, and neobanks, they face both unprecedented opportunities and critical challenges in areas such as data privacy, cybersecurity, and regulatory compliance. Futuristic banking represents a transformative shift in the global financial landscape, driven by innovations in digital technology, artificial intelligence, blockchain, and evolving consumer expectations. As traditional banks adapt to the rise of decentralized finance (DeFi), digital currencies, and neobanks, they face both unprecedented opportunities and critical challenges in areas such as data privacy, cybersecurity, and regulatory compliance. Futuristic banking represents a transformative shift in the global financial landscape, driven by innovations in digital technology, artificial intelligence, blockchain, and evolving consumer expectations. As traditional banks adapt to the rise of decentralized finance (DeFi), digital currencies, and neobanks, they face both unprecedented opportunities and critical challenges in areas such as data privacy, cybersecurity, and regulatory compliance. Futuristic banking represents a transformative shift in the global financial landscape, driven by innovations in digital technology, artificial intelligence, blockchain, and evolving consumer expectations. As traditional banks adapt to the rise of decentralized finance (DeFi), digital currencies, and neobanks, they face both unprecedented opportunities and critical challenges in areas such as data privacy, cybersecurity, and regulatory compliance. Futuristic banking represents a transformative shift in the global financial landscape, driven by innovations in digital technology, artificial intelligence, blockchain, and evolving consumer expectations. As traditional banks adapt to the rise of decentralized finance (DeFi), digital currencies, and neobanks, they face both unprecedented opportunities and critical challenges in areas such as data privacy, cybersecurity, and regulatory compliance. Futuristic banking represents a transformative shift in the global financial landscape, driven by innovations in digital technology, artificial intelligence, blockchain, and evolving consumer expectations. As traditional banks adapt to the rise of decentralized finance (DeFi), digital currencies, and neobanks, they face both unprecedented opportunities and critical challenges in areas such as data privacy, cybersecurity, and regulatory compliance. Futuristic banking represents a transformative shift in the global financial landscape, driven by innovations in digital technology, artificial intelligence, blockchain, and evolving consumer expectations. As traditional banks adapt to the rise of decentralized finance (DeFi), digital currencies, and neobanks, they face both unprecedented opportunities and critical challenges in areas such as data privacy, cybersecurity, and regulatory compliance. Futuristic banking represents a transformative shift in the global financial landscape, driven by innovations in digital technology, artificial intelligence, blockchain, and evolving consumer expectations. As traditional banks adapt to the rise of decentralized finance (DeFi), digital currencies, and neobanks, they face both unprecedented opportunities and critical challenges in areas such as data privacy, cybersecurity, and regulatory compliance. Futuristic banking represents a transformative shift in the global financial landscape, driven by innovations in digital technology, artificial intelligence, blockchain, and evolving consumer expectations. As traditional banks adapt to the rise of decentralized finance (DeFi), digital currencies, and neobanks, they face both unprecedented opportunities and critical challenges in areas such as data privacy, cybersecurity, and regulatory compliance. Futuristic banking represents a transformative shift in the global financial landscape, driven by innovations in digital technology, artificial intelligence, blockchain, and evolving consumer expectations. As traditional banks adapt to the rise of decentralized finance (DeFi), digital currencies, and neobanks, they face both unprecedented opportunities and critical challenges in areas such as data privacy, cybersecurity, and regulatory compliance. Futuristic banking represents a transformative shift in the global financial landscape, driven by innovations in digital technology, artificial intelligence, blockchain, and evolving consumer expectations. As traditional banks adapt to the rise of decentralized finance (DeFi), digital currencies, and neobanks, they face both unprecedented opportunities and critical challenges in areas such as data privacy, cybersecurity, and regulatory compliance. Futuristic banking represents a transformative shift in the global financial landscape, driven by innovations in digital technology, artificial intelligence, blockchain, and evolving consumer expectations. As traditional banks adapt to the rise of decentralized finance (DeFi), digital currencies, and neobanks, they face both unprecedented opportunities and critical challenges in areas such as data privacy, cybersecurity, and regulatory compliance. Futuristic banking represents a transformative shift in the global financial landscape, driven by innovations in digital technology, artificial intelligence, blockchain, and evolving consumer expectations. As traditional banks adapt to the rise of decentralized finance (DeFi), digital currencies, and neobanks, they face both unprecedented opportunities and critical challenges in areas such as data privacy, cybersecurity, and regulatory compliance. Futuristic banking represents a transformative shift in the global financial landscape, driven by innovations in digital technology, artificial intelligence, blockchain, and evolving consumer expectations. As traditional banks adapt to the rise of decentralized finance (DeFi), digital currencies, and neobanks, they face both unprecedented opportunities and critical challenges in areas such as data privacy, cybersecurity, and regulatory compliance. Futuristic banking represents a transformative shift in the global financial landscape, driven by innovations in digital technology, artificial intelligence, blockchain, and evolving consumer expectations. As traditional banks adapt to the rise of decentralized finance (DeFi), digital currencies, and neobanks, they face both unprecedented opportunities and critical challenges in areas such as data privacy, cybersecurity, and regulatory compliance. Futuristic banking represents a transformative shift in the global financial landscape, driven by innovations in digital technology, artificial intelligence, blockchain, and evolving consumer expectations. As traditional banks adapt to the rise of decentralized finance (DeFi), digital currencies, and neobanks, they face both unprecedented opportunities and critical challenges in areas such as data privacy, cybersecurity, and regulatory compliance. Futuristic banking represents a transformative shift in the global financial landscape, driven by innovations in digital technology, artificial intelligence, blockchain, and evolving consumer expectations. As traditional banks adapt to the rise of decentralized finance (DeFi), digital currencies, and neobanks, they face both unprecedented opportunities and critical challenges in areas such as data privacy, cybersecurity, and regulatory compliance. Futuristic banking represents a transformative shift in the global financial landscape, driven by innovations in digital technology, artificial intelligence, blockchain, and evolving consumer expectations. As traditional banks adapt to the rise of decentralized finance (DeFi), digital currencies, and neobanks, they face both unprecedented opportunities and critical challenges in areas such as data privacy, cybersecurity, and regulatory compliance. Futuristic banking represents a transformative shift in the global financial landscape, driven by innovations in digital technology, artificial intelligence, blockchain, and evolving consumer expectations. As traditional banks adapt to the rise of decentralized finance (DeFi), digital currencies, and neobanks, they face both unprecedented opportunities and critical challenges in areas such as data privacy, cybersecurity, and regulatory compliance. Futuristic banking represents a transformative shift in the global financial landscape, driven by innovations in digital technology, artificial intelligence, blockchain, and evolving consumer expectations. As traditional banks adapt to the rise of decentralized finance (DeFi), digital currencies, and neobanks, they face both unprecedented opportunities and critical challenges in areas such as data privacy, cybersecurity, and regulatory compliance. Futuristic banking represents a transformative shift in the global financial landscape, driven by innovations in digital technology, artificial intelligence, blockchain, and evolving consumer expectations. As traditional banks adapt to the rise of decentralized finance (DeFi), digital currencies, and neobanks, they face both unprecedented opportunities and critical challenges in areas such as data privacy, cybersecurity, and regulatory compliance. Futuristic banking represents a transformative shift in the global financial landscape, driven by innovations in digital technology, artificial intelligence, blockchain, and evolving consumer expectations. As traditional banks adapt to the rise of decentralized finance (DeFi), digital currencies, and neobanks, they face both unprecedented opportunities and critical challenges in areas such as data privacy, cybersecurity, and regulatory compliance. Futuristic banking represents a transformative shift in the global financial landscape, driven by innovations in digital technology, artificial intelligence, blockchain, and evolving consumer expectations. As traditional banks adapt to the rise of decentralized finance (DeFi), digital currencies, and neobanks, they face both unprecedented opportunities and critical challenges in areas such as data privacy, cybersecurity, and regulatory compliance. Futuristic banking represents a transformative shift in the global financial landscape, driven by innovations in digital technology, artificial intelligence, blockchain, and evolving consumer expectations. As traditional banks adapt to the rise of decentralized finance (DeFi), digital currencies, and neobanks, they face both unprecedented opportunities and critical challenges in areas such as data privacy, cybersecurity, and regulatory compliance. Futuristic banking represents a transformative shift in the global financial landscape, driven by innovations in digital technology, artificial intelligence, blockchain, and evolving consumer expectations. As traditional banks adapt to the rise of decentralized finance (DeFi), digital currencies, and neobanks, they face both unprecedented opportunities and critical challenges in areas such as data privacy, cybersecurity, and regulatory compliance. Futuristic banking represents a transformative shift in the global financial landscape, driven by innovations in digital technology, artificial intelligence, blockchain, and evolving consumer expectations. As traditional banks adapt to the rise of decentralized finance (DeFi), digital currencies, and neobanks, they face both unprecedented opportunities and critical challenges in areas such as data privacy, cybersecurity, and regulatory compliance. Futuristic banking represents a transformative shift in the global financial landscape, driven by innovations in digital technology, artificial intelligence, blockchain, and evolving consumer expectations. As traditional banks adapt to the rise of decentralized finance (DeFi), digital currencies, and neobanks, they face both unprecedented opportunities and critical challenges in areas such as data privacy, cybersecurity, and regulatory compliance. Futuristic banking represents a transformative shift in the global financial landscape, driven by innovations in digital technology, artificial intelligence, blockchain, and evolving consumer expectations. As traditional banks adapt to the rise of decentralized finance (DeFi), digital currencies, and neobanks, they face both unprecedented opportunities and critical challenges in areas such as data privacy, cybersecurity, and regulatory compliance. Futuristic banking represents a transformative shift in the global financial landscape, driven by innovations in digital technology, artificial intelligence, blockchain, and evolving consumer expectations. As traditional banks adapt to the rise of decentralized finance (DeFi), digital currencies, and neobanks, they face both unprecedented opportunities and critical challenges in areas such as data privacy, cybersecurity, and regulatory compliance. Futuristic banking represents a transformative shift in the global financial landscape, driven by innovations in digital technology, artificial intelligence, blockchain, and evolving consumer expectations. As traditional banks adapt to the rise of decentralized finance (DeFi), digital currencies, and neobanks, they face both unprecedented opportunities and critical challenges in areas such as data privacy, cybersecurity, and regulatory compliance. Futuristic banking represents a transformative shift in the global financial landscape, driven by innovations in digital technology, artificial intelligence, blockchain, and evolving consumer expectations. As traditional banks adapt to the rise of decentralized finance (DeFi), digital currencies, and neobanks, they face both unprecedented opportunities and critical challenges in areas such as data privacy, cybersecurity, and regulatory compliance. Futuristic banking represents a transformative shift in the global financial landscape, driven by innovations in digital technology, artificial intelligence, blockchain, and evolving consumer expectations. As traditional banks adapt to the rise of decentralized finance (DeFi), digital currencies, and neobanks, they face both unprecedented opportunities and critical challenges in areas such as data privacy, cybersecurity, and regulatory compliance. Futuristic banking represents a transformative shift in the global financial landscape, driven by innovations in digital technology, artificial intelligence, blockchain, and evolving consumer expectations. As traditional banks adapt to the rise of decentralized finance (DeFi), digital currencies, and neobanks, they face both unprecedented opportunities and critical challenges in areas such as data privacy, cybersecurity, and regulatory compliance. Futuristic banking represents a transformative shift in the global financial landscape, driven by innovations in digital technology, artificial intelligence, blockchain, and evolving consumer expectations. As traditional banks adapt to the rise of decentralized finance (DeFi), digital currencies, and neobanks, they face both unprecedented opportunities and critical challenges in areas such as data privacy, cybersecurity, and regulatory compliance. Futuristic banking represents a transformative shift in the global financial landscape, driven by innovations in digital technology, artificial intelligence, blockchain, and evolving consumer expectations. As traditional banks adapt to the rise of decentralized finance (DeFi), digital currencies, and neobanks, they face both unprecedented opportunities and critical challenges in areas such as data privacy, cybersecurity, and regulatory compliance. Futuristic banking represents a transformative shift in the global financial landscape, driven by innovations in digital technology, artificial intelligence, blockchain, and evolving consumer expectations. As traditional banks adapt to the rise of decentralized finance (DeFi), digital currencies, and neobanks, they face both unprecedented opportunities and critical challenges in areas such as data privacy, cybersecurity, and regulatory compliance. Futuristic banking represents a transformative shift in the global financial landscape, driven by innovations in digital technology, artificial intelligence, blockchain, and evolving consumer expectations. As traditional banks adapt to the rise of decentralized finance (DeFi), digital currencies, and neobanks, they face both unprecedented opportunities and critical challenges in areas such as data privacy, cybersecurity, and regulatory compliance. Futuristic banking represents a transformative shift in the global financial landscape, driven by innovations in digital technology, artificial intelligence, blockchain, and evolving consumer expectations. As traditional banks adapt to the rise of decentralized finance (DeFi), digital currencies, and neobanks, they face both unprecedented opportunities and critical challenges in areas such as data privacy, cybersecurity, and regulatory compliance. Futuristic banking represents a transformative shift in the global financial landscape, driven by innovations in digital technology, artificial intelligence, blockchain, and evolving consumer expectations. As traditional banks adapt to the rise of decentralized finance (DeFi), digital currencies, and neobanks, they face both unprecedented opportunities and critical challenges in areas such as data privacy, cybersecurity, and regulatory compliance. Futuristic banking represents a transformative shift in the global financial landscape, driven by innovations in digital technology, artificial intelligence, blockchain, and evolving consumer expectations. As traditional banks adapt to the rise of decentralized finance (DeFi), digital currencies, and neobanks, they face both unprecedented opportunities and critical challenges in areas such as data privacy, cybersecurity, and regulatory compliance. Futuristic banking represents a transformative shift in the global financial landscape, driven by innovations in digital technology, artificial intelligence, blockchain, and evolving consumer expectations. As traditional banks adapt to the rise of decentralized finance (DeFi), digital currencies, and neobanks, they face both unprecedented opportunities and critical challenges in areas such as data privacy, cybersecurity, and regulatory compliance. Futuristic banking represents a transformative shift in the global financial landscape, driven by innovations in digital technology, artificial intelligence, blockchain, and evolving consumer expectations. As traditional banks adapt to the rise of decentralized finance (DeFi), digital currencies, and neobanks, they face both unprecedented opportunities and critical challenges in areas such as data privacy, cybersecurity, and regulatory compliance. Futuristic banking represents a transformative shift in the global financial landscape, driven by innovations in digital technology, artificial intelligence, blockchain, and evolving consumer expectations. As traditional banks adapt to the rise of decentralized finance (DeFi), digital currencies, and neobanks, they face both unprecedented opportunities and critical challenges in areas such as data privacy, cybersecurity, and regulatory compliance. Futuristic banking represents a transformative shift in the global financial landscape, driven by innovations in digital technology, artificial intelligence, blockchain, and evolving consumer expectations. As traditional banks adapt to the rise of decentralized finance (DeFi), digital currencies, and neobanks, they face both unprecedented opportunities and critical challenges in areas such as data privacy, cybersecurity, and regulatory compliance. Futuristic banking represents a transformative shift in the global financial landscape, driven by innovations in digital technology, artificial intelligence, blockchain, and evolving consumer expectations. As traditional banks adapt to the rise of decentralized finance (DeFi), digital currencies, and neobanks, they face both unprecedented opportunities and critical challenges in areas such as data privacy, cybersecurity, and regulatory compliance. Futuristic banking represents a transformative shift in the global financial landscape, driven by innovations in digital technology, artificial intelligence, blockchain, and evolving consumer expectations. As traditional banks adapt to the rise of decentralized finance (DeFi), digital currencies, and neobanks, they face both unprecedented opportunities and critical challenges in areas such as data privacy, cybersecurity, and regulatory compliance. Futuristic banking represents a transformative shift in the global financial landscape, driven by innovations in digital technology, artificial intelligence, blockchain, and evolving consumer expectations. As traditional banks adapt to the rise of decentralized finance (DeFi), digital currencies, and neobanks, they face both unprecedented opportunities and critical challenges in areas such as data privacy, cybersecurity, and regulatory compliance. Futuristic banking represents a transformative shift in the global financial landscape, driven by innovations in digital technology, artificial intelligence, blockchain, and evolving consumer expectations. As traditional banks adapt to the rise of decentralized finance (DeFi), digital currencies, and neobanks, they face both unprecedented opportunities and critical challenges in areas such as data privacy, cybersecurity, and regulatory compliance. Futuristic banking represents a transformative shift in the global financial landscape, driven by innovations in digital technology, artificial intelligence, blockchain, and evolving consumer expectations. As traditional banks adapt to the rise of decentralized finance (DeFi), digital currencies, and neobanks, they face both unprecedented opportunities and critical challenges in areas such as data privacy, cybersecurity, and regulatory compliance. Futuristic banking represents a transformative shift in the global financial landscape, driven by innovations in digital technology, artificial intelligence, blockchain, and evolving consumer expectations. As traditional banks adapt to the rise of decentralized finance (DeFi), digital currencies, and neobanks, they face both unprecedented opportunities and critical challenges in areas such as data privacy, cybersecurity, and regulatory compliance. Futuristic banking represents a transformative shift in the global financial landscape, driven by innovations in digital technology, artificial intelligence, blockchain, and evolving consumer expectations. As traditional banks adapt to the rise of decentralized finance (DeFi), digital currencies, and neobanks, they face both unprecedented opportunities and critical challenges in areas such as data privacy, cybersecurity, and regulatory compliance. Futuristic banking represents a transformative shift in the global financial landscape, driven by innovations in digital technology, artificial intelligence, blockchain, and evolving consumer expectations. As traditional banks adapt to the rise of decentralized finance (DeFi), digital currencies, and neobanks, they face both unprecedented opportunities and critical challenges in areas such as data privacy, cybersecurity, and regulatory compliance. Futuristic banking represents a transformative shift in the global financial landscape, driven by innovations in digital technology, artificial intelligence, blockchain, and evolving consumer expectations. As traditional banks adapt to the rise of decentralized finance (DeFi), digital currencies, and neobanks, they face both unprecedented opportunities and critical challenges in areas such as data privacy, cybersecurity, and regulatory compliance. Futuristic banking represents a transformative shift in the global financial landscape, driven by innovations in digital technology, artificial intelligence, blockchain, and evolving consumer expectations. As traditional banks adapt to the rise of decentralized finance (DeFi), digital currencies, and neobanks, they face both unprecedented opportunities and critical challenges in areas such as data privacy, cybersecurity, and regulatory compliance. Futuristic banking represents a transformative shift in the global financial landscape, driven by innovations in digital technology, artificial intelligence, blockchain, and evolving consumer expectations. As traditional banks adapt to the rise of decentralized finance (DeFi), digital currencies, and neobanks, they face both unprecedented opportunities and critical challenges in areas such as data privacy, cybersecurity, and regulatory compliance. Futuristic banking represents a transformative shift in the global financial landscape, driven by innovations in digital technology, artificial intelligence, blockchain, and evolving consumer expectations. As traditional banks adapt to the rise of decentralized finance (DeFi), digital currencies, and neobanks, they face both unprecedented opportunities and critical challenges in areas such as data privacy, cybersecurity, and regulatory compliance. Futuristic banking represents a transformative shift in the global financial landscape, driven by innovations in digital technology, artificial intelligence, blockchain, and evolving consumer expectations. As traditional banks adapt to the rise of decentralized finance (DeFi), digital currencies, and neobanks, they face both unprecedented opportunities and critical challenges in areas such as data privacy, cybersecurity, and regulatory compliance. Futuristic banking represents a transformative shift in the global financial landscape, driven by innovations in digital technology, artificial intelligence, blockchain, and evolving consumer expectations. As traditional banks adapt to the rise of decentralized finance (DeFi), digital currencies, and neobanks, they face both unprecedented opportunities and critical challenges in areas such as data privacy, cybersecurity, and regulatory compliance. Futuristic banking represents a transformative shift in the global financial landscape, driven by innovations in digital technology, artificial intelligence, blockchain, and evolving consumer expectations. As traditional banks adapt to the rise of decentralized finance (DeFi), digital currencies, and neobanks, they face both unprecedented opportunities and critical challenges in areas such as data privacy, cybersecurity, and regulatory compliance. Futuristic banking represents a transformative shift in the global financial landscape, driven by innovations in digital technology, artificial intelligence, blockchain, and evolving consumer expectations. As traditional banks adapt to the rise of decentralized finance (DeFi), digital currencies, and neobanks, they face both unprecedented opportunities and critical challenges in areas such as data privacy, cybersecurity, and regulatory compliance. Futuristic banking represents a transformative shift in the global financial landscape, driven by innovations in digital technology, artificial intelligence, blockchain, and evolving consumer expectations. As traditional banks adapt to the rise of decentralized finance (DeFi), digital currencies, and neobanks, they face both unprecedented opportunities and critical challenges in areas such as data privacy, cybersecurity, and regulatory compliance. Futuristic banking represents a transformative shift in the global financial landscape, driven by innovations in digital technology, artificial intelligence, blockchain, and evolving consumer expectations. As traditional banks adapt to the rise of decentralized finance (DeFi), digital currencies, and neobanks, they face both unprecedented opportunities and critical challenges in areas such as data privacy, cybersecurity, and regulatory compliance. Futuristic banking represents a transformative shift in the global financial landscape, driven by innovations in digital technology, artificial intelligence, blockchain, and evolving consumer expectations. As traditional banks adapt to the rise of decentralized finance (DeFi), digital currencies, and neobanks, they face both unprecedented opportunities and critical challenges in areas such as data privacy, cybersecurity, and regulatory compliance. Futuristic banking represents a transformative shift in the global financial landscape, driven by innovations in digital technology, artificial intelligence, blockchain, and evolving consumer expectations. As traditional banks adapt to the rise of decentralized finance (DeFi), digital currencies, and neobanks, they face both unprecedented opportunities and critical challenges in areas such as data privacy, cybersecurity, and regulatory compliance. Futuristic banking represents a transformative shift in the global financial landscape, driven by innovations in digital technology, artificial intelligence, blockchain, and evolving consumer expectations. As traditional banks adapt to the rise of decentralized finance (DeFi), digital currencies, and neobanks, they face both unprecedented opportunities and critical challenges in areas such as data privacy, cybersecurity, and regulatory compliance. Futuristic banking represents a transformative shift in the global financial landscape, driven by innovations in digital technology, artificial intelligence, blockchain, and evolving consumer expectations. As traditional banks adapt to the rise of decentralized finance (DeFi), digital currencies, and neobanks, they face both unprecedented opportunities and critical challenges in areas such as data privacy, cybersecurity, and regulatory compliance. Futuristic banking represents a transformative shift in the global financial landscape, driven by innovations in digital technology, artificial intelligence, blockchain, and evolving consumer expectations. As traditional banks adapt to the rise of decentralized finance (DeFi), digital currencies, and neobanks, they face both unprecedented opportunities and critical challenges in areas such as data privacy, cybersecurity, and regulatory compliance. Futuristic banking represents a transformative shift in the global financial landscape, driven by innovations in digital technology, artificial intelligence, blockchain, and evolving consumer expectations. As traditional banks adapt to the rise of decentralized finance (DeFi), digital currencies, and neobanks, they face both unprecedented opportunities and critical challenges in areas such as data privacy, cybersecurity, and regulatory compliance. Futuristic banking represents a transformative shift in the global financial landscape, driven by innovations in digital technology, artificial intelligence, blockchain, and evolving consumer expectations. As traditional banks adapt to the rise of decentralized finance (DeFi), digital currencies, and neobanks, they face both unprecedented opportunities and critical challenges in areas such as data privacy, cybersecurity, and regulatory compliance. Futuristic banking represents a transformative shift in the global financial landscape, driven by innovations in digital technology, artificial intelligence, blockchain, and evolving consumer expectations. As traditional banks adapt to the rise of decentralized finance (DeFi), digital currencies, and neobanks, they face both unprecedented opportunities and critical challenges in areas such as data privacy, cybersecurity, and regulatory compliance. Futuristic banking represents a transformative shift.

Global Recession and the Banking Sector's Role: A Unified Summary

The global economy has experienced several significant recessions throughout history, many of which were either triggered or exacerbated by the banking sector. From the Great Depression in 1929 to the Global Financial Crisis in 2008, banks have played a pivotal role in shaping the trajectory of economic growth and collapse. Poor regulation, excessive risk-taking, and a lack of transparency have often been at the heart of financial disasters. For instance, in 2008, the collapse of Lehman Brothers symbolized the failure of regulatory oversight and the systemic vulnerabilities within the global banking system. The repercussions were catastrophic: millions of people lost their jobs, homes, and savings. Central banks had to intervene on a massive scale, implementing quantitative easing and slashing interest rates to stabilize markets. More recently, the COVID-19 pandemic tested the resilience of banks, which, under tighter regulations post-2008, proved more robust. However, new challenges such as inflation, war, and digital disruptions continue to pose threats to economic stability. The global economy has experienced several significant recessions throughout history, many of which were either triggered or exacerbated by the banking sector. From the Great Depression in 1929 to the Global Financial Crisis in 2008, banks have played a pivotal role in shaping the trajectory of economic growth and collapse. Poor regulation, excessive risk-taking, and a lack of transparency have often been at the heart of financial disasters. For instance, in 2008, the collapse of Lehman Brothers symbolized the failure of regulatory oversight and the systemic vulnerabilities within the global banking system. The repercussions were catastrophic: millions of people lost their jobs, homes, and savings. Central banks had to intervene on a massive scale, implementing quantitative easing and slashing interest rates to stabilize markets. More recently, the COVID-19 pandemic tested the resilience of banks, which, under tighter regulations post-2008, proved more robust. However, new challenges such as inflation, war, and digital disruptions continue to pose threats to economic stability. The global economy has experienced several significant recessions throughout history, many of which were either triggered or exacerbated by the banking sector. From the Great Depression in 1929 to the Global Financial Crisis in 2008, banks have played a pivotal role in shaping the trajectory of economic growth and collapse. Poor regulation, excessive risk-taking, and a lack of transparency have often been at the heart of financial disasters. For instance, in 2008, the collapse of Lehman Brothers symbolized the failure of regulatory oversight and the systemic vulnerabilities within the global banking system. The repercussions were catastrophic: millions of people lost their jobs, homes, and savings. Central banks had to intervene on a massive scale, implementing quantitative easing and slashing interest rates to stabilize markets. More recently, the COVID-19 pandemic tested the resilience of banks, which, under tighter regulations post-2008, proved more robust. However, new challenges such as inflation, war, and digital disruptions continue to pose threats to economic stability. The global economy has experienced several significant recessions throughout history, many of which were either triggered or exacerbated by the banking sector. From the Great Depression in 1929 to the Global Financial Crisis in 2008, banks have played a pivotal role in shaping the trajectory of economic growth and collapse. Poor regulation, excessive risk-taking, and a lack of transparency have often been at the heart of financial disasters. For instance, in 2008, the collapse of Lehman Brothers symbolized the failure of regulatory oversight and the systemic vulnerabilities within the global banking system. The repercussions were catastrophic: millions of people lost their jobs, homes, and savings. Central banks had to intervene on a massive scale, implementing quantitative easing and slashing interest rates to stabilize markets. More recently, the COVID-19 pandemic tested the resilience of banks, which, under tighter regulations post-2008, proved more robust. However, new challenges such as inflation, war, and digital disruptions continue to pose threats to economic stability. The global economy has experienced several significant recessions throughout history, many of which were either triggered or exacerbated by the banking sector. From the Great Depression in 1929 to the Global Financial Crisis in 2008, banks have played a pivotal role in shaping the trajectory of economic growth and collapse. Poor regulation, excessive risk-taking, and a lack of transparency have often been at the heart of financial disasters. For instance, in 2008, the collapse of Lehman Brothers symbolized the failure of regulatory oversight and the systemic vulnerabilities within the global banking system. The repercussions were catastrophic: millions of people lost their jobs, homes, and savings. Central banks had to intervene on a massive scale, implementing quantitative easing and slashing interest rates to stabilize markets. More recently, the COVID-19 pandemic tested the resilience of banks, which, under tighter regulations post-2008, proved more robust. However, new challenges such as inflation, war, and digital disruptions continue to pose threats to economic stability. The global economy has experienced several significant recessions throughout history, many of which were either triggered or exacerbated by the banking sector. From the Great Depression in 1929 to the Global Financial Crisis in 2008, banks have played a pivotal role in shaping the trajectory of economic growth and collapse. Poor regulation, excessive risk-taking, and a lack of transparency have often been at the heart of financial disasters. For instance, in 2008, the collapse of Lehman Brothers symbolized the failure of regulatory oversight and the systemic vulnerabilities within the global banking system. The repercussions were catastrophic: millions of people lost their jobs, homes, and savings. Central banks had to intervene on a massive scale, implementing quantitative easing and slashing interest rates to stabilize markets. More recently, the COVID-19 pandemic tested the resilience of banks, which, under tighter regulations post-2008, proved more robust. However, new challenges such as inflation, war, and digital disruptions continue to pose threats to economic stability. The global economy has experienced several significant recessions throughout history, many of which were either triggered or exacerbated by the banking sector. From the Great Depression in 1929 to the Global Financial Crisis in 2008, banks have played a pivotal role in shaping the trajectory of economic growth and collapse. Poor regulation, excessive risk-taking, and a lack of transparency have often been at the heart of financial disasters. For instance, in 2008, the collapse of Lehman Brothers symbolized the failure of regulatory oversight and the systemic vulnerabilities within the global banking system. The repercussions were catastrophic: millions of people lost their jobs, homes, and savings. Central banks had to intervene on a massive scale, implementing quantitative easing and slashing interest rates to stabilize markets. More recently, the COVID-19 pandemic tested the resilience of banks, which, under tighter regulations post-2008, proved more robust. However, new challenges such as inflation, war, and digital disruptions continue to pose threats to economic stability. The global economy has experienced several significant recessions throughout history, many of which were either triggered or exacerbated by the banking sector. From the Great Depression in 1929 to the Global Financial Crisis in 2008, banks have played a pivotal role in shaping the trajectory of economic growth and collapse. Poor regulation, excessive risk-taking, and a lack of transparency have often been at the heart of financial disasters. For instance, in 2008, the collapse of Lehman Brothers symbolized the failure of regulatory oversight and the systemic vulnerabilities within the global banking system. The repercussions were catastrophic: millions of people lost their jobs, homes, and savings. Central banks had to intervene on a massive scale, implementing quantitative easing and slashing interest rates to stabilize markets. More recently, the COVID-19 pandemic tested the resilience of banks, which, under tighter regulations post-2008, proved more robust. However, new challenges such as inflation, war, and digital disruptions continue to pose threats to economic stability. The global economy has experienced several significant recessions throughout history, many of which were either triggered or exacerbated by the banking sector. From the Great Depression in 1929 to the Global Financial Crisis in 2008, banks have played a pivotal role in shaping the trajectory of economic growth and collapse. Poor regulation, excessive risk-taking, and a lack of transparency have often been at the heart of financial disasters. For instance, in 2008, the collapse of Lehman Brothers symbolized the failure of regulatory oversight and the systemic vulnerabilities within the global banking system. The repercussions were catastrophic: millions of people lost their jobs, homes, and savings. Central banks had to intervene on a massive scale, implementing quantitative easing and slashing interest rates to stabilize markets. More recently, the COVID-19 pandemic tested the resilience of banks, which, under tighter regulations post-2008, proved more robust. However, new challenges such as inflation, war, and digital disruptions continue to pose threats to economic stability. The global economy has experienced several significant recessions throughout history, many of which were either triggered or exacerbated by the banking sector. From the Great Depression in 1929 to the Global Financial Crisis in 2008, banks have played a pivotal role in shaping the trajectory of economic growth and collapse. Poor regulation, excessive risk-taking, and a lack of transparency have often been at the heart of financial disasters. For instance, in 2008, the collapse of Lehman Brothers symbolized the failure of regulatory oversight and the systemic vulnerabilities within the global banking system. The repercussions were catastrophic: millions of people lost their jobs, homes, and savings. Central banks had to intervene on a massive scale, implementing quantitative easing and slashing interest rates to stabilize markets. More recently, the COVID-19 pandemic tested the resilience of banks, which, under tighter regulations post-2008, proved more robust. However, new challenges such as inflation, war, and digital disruptions continue to pose threats to economic stability. The global economy has experienced several significant recessions throughout history, many of which were either triggered or exacerbated by the banking sector. From the Great Depression in 1929 to the Global Financial Crisis in 2008, banks have played a pivotal role in shaping the trajectory of economic growth and collapse. Poor regulation, excessive risk-taking, and a lack of transparency have often been at the heart of financial disasters. For instance, in 2008, the collapse of Lehman Brothers symbolized the failure of regulatory oversight and the systemic vulnerabilities within the global banking system. The repercussions were catastrophic: millions of people lost their jobs, homes, and savings. Central banks had to intervene on a massive scale, implementing quantitative easing and slashing interest rates to stabilize markets. More recently, the COVID-19 pandemic tested the resilience of banks, which, under tighter regulations post-2008, proved more robust. However, new challenges such as inflation, war, and digital disruptions continue to pose threats to economic stability. The global economy has experienced several significant recessions throughout history, many of which were either triggered or exacerbated by the banking sector. From the Great Depression in 1929 to the Global Financial Crisis in 2008, banks have played a pivotal role in shaping the trajectory of economic growth and collapse. Poor regulation, excessive risk-taking, and a lack of transparency have often been at the heart of financial disasters. For instance, in 2008, the collapse of Lehman Brothers symbolized the failure of regulatory oversight and the systemic vulnerabilities within the global banking system. The repercussions were catastrophic: millions of people lost their jobs, homes, and savings. Central banks had to intervene on a massive scale, implementing quantitative easing and slashing interest rates to stabilize markets. More recently, the COVID-19 pandemic tested the resilience of banks, which, under tighter regulations post-2008, proved more robust. However, new challenges such as inflation, war, and digital disruptions continue to pose threats to economic stability. The global economy has experienced several significant recessions throughout history, many of which were either triggered or exacerbated by the banking sector. From the Great Depression in 1929 to the Global Financial Crisis in 2008, banks have played a pivotal role in shaping the trajectory of economic growth and collapse. Poor regulation, excessive risk-taking, and a lack of transparency have often been at the heart of financial disasters. For instance, in 2008, the collapse of Lehman Brothers symbolized the failure of regulatory oversight and the systemic vulnerabilities within the global banking system. The repercussions were catastrophic: millions of people lost their jobs, homes, and savings. Central banks had to intervene on a massive scale, implementing quantitative easing and slashing interest rates to stabilize markets. More recently, the COVID-19 pandemic tested the resilience of banks, which, under tighter regulations post-2008, proved more robust. However, new challenges such as inflation, war, and digital disruptions continue to pose threats to economic stability. The global economy has experienced several significant recessions throughout history, many of which were either triggered or exacerbated by the banking sector. From the Great Depression in 1929 to the Global Financial Crisis in 2008, banks have played a pivotal role in shaping the trajectory of economic growth and collapse. Poor regulation, excessive risk-taking, and a lack of transparency have often been at the heart of financial disasters. For instance, in 2008, the collapse of Lehman Brothers symbolized the failure of regulatory oversight and the systemic vulnerabilities within the global banking system. The repercussions were catastrophic: millions of people lost their jobs, homes, and savings. Central banks had to intervene on a massive scale, implementing quantitative easing and slashing interest rates to stabilize markets. More recently, the COVID-19 pandemic tested the resilience of banks, which, under tighter regulations post-2008, proved more robust. However, new challenges such as inflation, war, and digital disruptions continue to pose threats to economic stability. The global economy has experienced several significant recessions throughout history, many of which were either triggered or exacerbated by the banking sector. From the Great Depression in 1929 to the Global Financial Crisis in 2008, banks have played a pivotal role in shaping the trajectory of economic growth and collapse. Poor regulation, excessive risk-taking, and a lack of transparency have often been at the heart of financial disasters. For instance, in 2008, the collapse of Lehman Brothers symbolized the failure of regulatory oversight and the systemic vulnerabilities within the global banking system. The repercussions were catastrophic: millions of people lost their jobs, homes, and savings. Central banks had to intervene on a massive scale, implementing quantitative easing and slashing interest rates to stabilize markets. More recently, the COVID-19 pandemic tested the resilience of banks, which, under tighter regulations post-2008, proved more robust. However, new challenges such as inflation, war, and digital disruptions continue to pose threats to economic stability. The global economy has experienced several significant recessions throughout history, many of which were either triggered or exacerbated by the banking sector. From the Great Depression in 1929 to the Global Financial Crisis in 2008, banks have played a pivotal role in shaping the trajectory of economic growth and collapse. Poor regulation, excessive risk-taking, and a lack of transparency have often been at the heart of financial disasters. For instance, in 2008, the collapse of Lehman Brothers symbolized the failure of regulatory oversight and the systemic vulnerabilities within the global banking system. The repercussions were catastrophic: millions of people lost their jobs, homes, and savings. Central banks had to intervene on a massive scale, implementing quantitative easing and slashing interest rates to stabilize markets. More recently, the COVID-19 pandemic tested the resilience of banks, which, under tighter regulations post-2008, proved more robust. However, new challenges such as inflation, war, and digital disruptions continue to pose threats to economic stability. The global economy has experienced several significant recessions throughout history, many of which were either triggered or exacerbated by the banking sector. From the Great Depression in 1929 to the Global Financial Crisis in 2008, banks have played a pivotal role in shaping the trajectory of economic growth and collapse. Poor regulation, excessive risk-taking, and a lack of transparency have often been at the heart of financial disasters. For instance, in 2008, the collapse of Lehman Brothers symbolized the failure of regulatory oversight and the systemic vulnerabilities within the global banking system. The repercussions were catastrophic: millions of people lost their jobs, homes, and savings. Central banks had to intervene on a massive scale, implementing quantitative easing and slashing interest rates to stabilize markets. More recently, the COVID-19 pandemic tested the resilience of banks, which, under tighter regulations post-2008, proved more robust. However, new challenges such as inflation, war, and digital disruptions continue to pose threats to economic stability. The global economy has experienced several significant recessions throughout history, many of which were either triggered or exacerbated by the banking sector. From the Great Depression in 1929 to the Global Financial Crisis in 2008, banks have played a pivotal role in shaping the trajectory of economic growth and collapse. Poor regulation, excessive risk-taking, and a lack of transparency have often been at the heart of financial disasters. For instance, in 2008, the collapse of Lehman Brothers symbolized the failure of regulatory oversight and the systemic vulnerabilities within the global banking system. The repercussions were catastrophic: millions of people lost their jobs, homes, and savings. Central banks had to intervene on a massive scale, implementing quantitative easing and slashing interest rates to stabilize markets. More recently, the COVID-19 pandemic tested the resilience of banks, which, under tighter regulations post-2008, proved more robust. However, new challenges such as inflation, war, and digital disruptions continue to pose threats to economic stability. The global economy has experienced several significant recessions throughout history, many of which were either triggered or exacerbated by the banking sector. From the Great Depression in 1929 to the Global Financial Crisis in 2008, banks have played a pivotal role in shaping the trajectory of economic growth and collapse. Poor regulation, excessive risk-taking, and a lack of transparency have often been at the heart of financial disasters. For instance, in 2008, the collapse of Lehman Brothers symbolized the failure of regulatory oversight and the systemic vulnerabilities within the global banking system. The repercussions were catastrophic: millions of people lost their jobs, homes, and savings. Central banks had to intervene on a massive scale, implementing quantitative easing and slashing interest rates to stabilize markets. More recently, the COVID-19 pandemic tested the resilience of banks, which, under tighter regulations post-2008, proved more robust. However, new challenges such as inflation, war, and digital disruptions continue to pose threats to economic stability. The global economy has experienced several significant recessions throughout history, many of which were either triggered or exacerbated by the banking sector. From the Great Depression in 1929 to the Global Financial Crisis in 2008, banks have played a pivotal role in shaping the trajectory of economic growth and collapse. Poor regulation, excessive risk-taking, and a lack of transparency have often been at the heart of financial disasters. For instance, in 2008, the collapse of Lehman Brothers symbolized the failure of regulatory oversight and the systemic vulnerabilities within the global banking system. The repercussions were catastrophic: millions of people lost their jobs, homes, and savings. Central banks had to intervene on a massive scale, implementing quantitative easing and slashing interest rates to stabilize markets. More recently, the COVID-19 pandemic tested the resilience of banks, which, under tighter regulations post-2008, proved more robust. However, new challenges such as inflation, war, and digital disruptions continue to pose threats to economic stability. The global economy has experienced several significant recessions throughout history, many of which were either triggered or exacerbated by the banking sector. From the Great Depression in 1929 to the Global Financial Crisis in 2008, banks have played a pivotal role in shaping the trajectory of economic growth and collapse. Poor regulation, excessive risk-taking, and a lack of transparency have often been at the heart of financial disasters. For instance, in 2008, the collapse of Lehman Brothers symbolized the failure of regulatory oversight and the systemic vulnerabilities within the global banking system. The repercussions were catastrophic: millions of people lost their jobs, homes, and savings. Central banks had to intervene on a massive scale, implementing quantitative easing and slashing interest rates to stabilize markets. More recently, the COVID-19 pandemic tested the resilience of banks, which, under tighter regulations post-2008, proved more robust. However, new challenges such as inflation, war, and digital disruptions continue to pose threats to economic stability. The global economy has experienced several significant recessions throughout history, many of which were either triggered or exacerbated by the banking sector. From the Great Depression in 1929 to the Global Financial Crisis in 2008, banks have played a pivotal role in shaping the trajectory of economic growth and collapse. Poor regulation, excessive risk-taking, and a lack of transparency have often been at the heart of financial disasters. For instance, in 2008, the collapse of Lehman Brothers symbolized the failure of regulatory oversight and the systemic vulnerabilities within the global banking system. The repercussions were catastrophic: millions of people lost their jobs, homes, and savings. Central banks had to intervene on a massive scale, implementing quantitative easing and slashing interest rates to stabilize markets. More recently, the COVID-19 pandemic tested the resilience of banks, which, under tighter regulations post-2008, proved more robust. However, new challenges such as inflation, war, and digital disruptions continue to pose threats to economic stability. The global economy has experienced several significant recessions throughout history, many of which were either triggered or exacerbated by the banking sector. From the Great Depression in 1929 to the Global Financial Crisis in 2008, banks have played a pivotal role in shaping the trajectory of economic growth and collapse. Poor regulation, excessive risk-taking, and a lack of transparency have often been at the heart of financial disasters. For instance, in 2008, the collapse of Lehman Brothers symbolized the failure of regulatory oversight and the systemic vulnerabilities within the global banking system. The repercussions were catastrophic: millions of people lost their jobs, homes, and savings. Central banks had to intervene on a massive scale, implementing quantitative easing and slashing interest rates to stabilize markets. More recently, the COVID-19 pandemic tested the resilience of banks, which, under tighter regulations post-2008, proved more robust. However, new challenges such as inflation, war, and digital disruptions continue to pose threats to economic stability. The global economy has experienced several significant recessions throughout history, many of which were either triggered or exacerbated by the banking sector. From the Great Depression in 1929 to the Global Financial Crisis in 2008, banks have played a pivotal role in shaping the trajectory of economic growth and collapse. Poor regulation, excessive risk-taking, and a lack of transparency have often been at the heart of financial disasters. For instance, in 2008, the collapse of Lehman Brothers symbolized the failure of regulatory oversight and the systemic vulnerabilities within the global banking system. The repercussions were catastrophic: millions of people lost their jobs, homes, and savings. Central banks had to intervene on a massive scale, implementing quantitative easing and slashing interest rates to stabilize markets. More recently, the COVID-19 pandemic tested the resilience of banks, which, under tighter regulations post-2008, proved more robust. However, new challenges such as inflation, war, and digital disruptions continue to pose threats to economic stability. The global economy has experienced several significant recessions throughout history, many of which were either triggered or exacerbated by the banking sector. From the Great Depression in 1929 to the Global Financial Crisis in 2008, banks have played a pivotal role in shaping the trajectory of economic growth and collapse. Poor regulation, excessive risk-taking, and a lack of transparency have often been at the heart of financial disasters. For instance, in 2008, the collapse of Lehman Brothers symbolized the failure of regulatory oversight and the systemic vulnerabilities within the global banking system. The repercussions were catastrophic: millions of people lost their jobs, homes, and savings. Central banks had to intervene on a massive scale, implementing quantitative easing and slashing interest rates to stabilize markets. More recently, the COVID-19 pandemic tested the resilience of banks, which, under tighter regulations post-2008, proved more robust. However, new challenges such as inflation, war, and digital disruptions continue to pose threats to economic stability. The global economy has experienced several significant recessions throughout history, many of which were either triggered or exacerbated by the banking sector. From the Great Depression in 1929 to the Global Financial Crisis in 2008, banks have played a pivotal role in shaping the trajectory of economic growth and collapse. Poor regulation, excessive risk-taking, and a lack of transparency have often been at the heart of financial disasters. For instance, in 2008, the collapse of Lehman Brothers symbolized the failure of regulatory oversight and the systemic vulnerabilities within the global banking system. The repercussions were catastrophic: millions of people lost their jobs, homes, and savings. Central banks had to intervene on a massive scale, implementing quantitative easing and slashing interest rates to stabilize markets. More recently, the COVID-19 pandemic tested the resilience of banks, which, under tighter regulations post-2008, proved more robust. However, new challenges such as inflation, war, and digital disruptions continue to pose threats to economic stability. The global economy has experienced several significant recessions throughout history, many of which were either triggered or exacerbated by the banking sector. From the Great Depression in 1929 to the Global Financial Crisis in 2008, banks have played a pivotal role in shaping the trajectory of economic growth and collapse. Poor regulation, excessive risk-taking, and a lack of transparency have often been at the heart of financial disasters. For instance, in 2008, the collapse of Lehman Brothers symbolized the failure of regulatory oversight and the systemic vulnerabilities within the global banking system. The repercussions were catastrophic: millions of people lost their jobs, homes, and savings. Central banks had to intervene on a massive scale, implementing quantitative easing and slashing interest rates to stabilize markets. More recently, the COVID-19 pandemic tested the resilience of banks, which, under tighter regulations post-2008, proved more robust. However, new challenges such as inflation, war, and digital disruptions continue to pose threats to economic stability. The global economy has experienced several significant recessions throughout history, many of which were either triggered or exacerbated by the banking sector. From the Great Depression in 1929 to the Global Financial Crisis in 2008, banks have played a pivotal role in shaping the trajectory of economic growth and collapse. Poor regulation, excessive risk-taking, and a lack of transparency have often been at the heart of financial disasters. For instance, in 2008, the collapse of Lehman Brothers symbolized the failure of regulatory oversight and the systemic vulnerabilities within the global banking system. The repercussions were catastrophic: millions of people lost their jobs, homes, and savings. Central banks had to intervene on a massive scale, implementing quantitative easing and slashing interest rates to stabilize markets. More recently, the COVID-19 pandemic tested the resilience of banks, which, under tighter regulations post-2008, proved more robust. However, new challenges such as inflation, war, and digital disruptions continue to pose threats to economic stability. The global economy has experienced several significant recessions throughout history, many of which were either triggered or exacerbated by the banking sector. From the Great Depression in 1929 to the Global Financial Crisis in 2008, banks have played a pivotal role in shaping the trajectory of economic growth and collapse. Poor regulation, excessive risk-taking, and a lack of transparency have often been at the heart of financial disasters. For instance, in 2008, the collapse of Lehman Brothers symbolized the failure of regulatory oversight and the systemic vulnerabilities within the global banking system. The repercussions were catastrophic: millions of people lost their jobs, homes, and savings. Central banks had to intervene on a massive scale, implementing quantitative easing and slashing interest rates to stabilize markets. More recently, the COVID-19 pandemic tested the resilience of banks, which, under tighter regulations post-2008, proved more robust. However, new challenges such as inflation, war, and digital disruptions continue to pose threats to economic stability. The global economy has experienced several significant recessions throughout history, many of which were either triggered or exacerbated by the banking sector. From the Great Depression in 1929 to the Global Financial Crisis in 2008, banks have played a pivotal role in shaping the trajectory of economic growth and collapse. Poor regulation, excessive risk-taking, and a lack of transparency have often been at the heart of financial disasters. For instance, in 2008, the collapse of Lehman Brothers symbolized the failure of regulatory oversight and the systemic vulnerabilities within the global banking system. The repercussions were catastrophic: millions of people lost their jobs, homes, and savings. Central banks had to intervene on a massive scale, implementing quantitative easing and slashing interest rates to stabilize markets. More recently, the COVID-19 pandemic tested the resilience of banks, which, under tighter regulations post-2008, proved more robust. However, new challenges such as inflation, war, and digital disruptions continue to pose threats to economic stability. The global economy has experienced several significant recessions throughout history, many of which were either triggered or exacerbated by the banking sector. From the Great Depression in 1929 to the Global Financial Crisis in 2008, banks have played a pivotal role in shaping the trajectory of economic growth and collapse. Poor regulation, excessive risk-taking, and a lack of transparency have often been at the heart of financial disasters. For instance, in 2008, the collapse of Lehman Brothers symbolized the failure of regulatory oversight and the systemic vulnerabilities within the global banking system. The repercussions were catastrophic: millions of people lost their jobs, homes, and savings. Central banks had to intervene on a massive scale, implementing quantitative easing and slashing interest rates to stabilize markets. More recently, the COVID-19 pandemic tested the resilience of banks, which, under tighter regulations post-2008, proved more robust. However, new challenges such as inflation, war, and digital disruptions continue to pose threats to economic stability. The global economy has experienced several significant recessions throughout history, many of which were either triggered or exacerbated by the banking sector. From the Great Depression in 1929 to the Global Financial Crisis in 2008, banks have played a pivotal role in shaping the trajectory of economic growth and collapse. Poor regulation, excessive risk-taking, and a lack of transparency have often been at the heart of financial disasters. For instance, in 2008, the collapse of Lehman Brothers symbolized the failure of regulatory oversight and the systemic vulnerabilities within the global banking system. The repercussions were catastrophic: millions of people lost their jobs, homes, and savings. Central banks had to intervene on a massive scale, implementing quantitative easing and slashing interest rates to stabilize markets. More recently, the COVID-19 pandemic tested the resilience of banks, which, under tighter regulations post-2008, proved more robust. However, new challenges such as inflation, war, and digital disruptions continue to pose threats to economic stability. The global economy has experienced several significant recessions throughout history, many of which were either triggered or exacerbated by the banking sector. From the Great Depression in 1929 to the Global Financial Crisis in 2008, banks have played a pivotal role in shaping the trajectory of economic growth and collapse. Poor regulation, excessive risk-taking, and a lack of transparency have often been at the heart of financial disasters. For instance, in 2008, the collapse of Lehman Brothers symbolized the failure of regulatory oversight and the systemic vulnerabilities within the global banking system. The repercussions were catastrophic: millions of people lost their jobs, homes, and savings. Central banks had to intervene on a massive scale, implementing quantitative easing and slashing interest rates to stabilize markets. More recently, the COVID-19 pandemic tested the resilience of banks, which, under tighter regulations post-2008, proved more robust. However, new challenges such as inflation, war, and digital disruptions continue to pose threats to economic stability. The global economy has experienced several significant recessions throughout history, many of which were either triggered or exacerbated by the banking sector. From the Great Depression in 1929 to the Global Financial Crisis in 2008, banks have played a pivotal role in shaping the trajectory of economic growth and collapse. Poor regulation, excessive risk-taking, and a lack of transparency have often been at the heart of financial disasters. For instance, in 2008, the collapse of Lehman Brothers symbolized the failure of regulatory oversight and the systemic vulnerabilities within the global banking system. The repercussions were catastrophic: millions of people lost their jobs, homes, and savings. Central banks had to intervene on a massive scale, implementing quantitative easing and slashing interest rates to stabilize markets. More recently, the COVID-19 pandemic tested the resilience of banks, which, under tighter regulations post-2008, proved more robust. However, new challenges such as inflation, war, and digital disruptions continue to pose threats to economic stability. The global economy has experienced several significant recessions throughout history, many of which were either triggered or exacerbated by the banking sector. From the Great Depression in 1929 to the Global Financial Crisis in 2008, banks have played a pivotal role in shaping the trajectory of economic growth and collapse. Poor regulation, excessive risk-taking, and a lack of transparency have often been at the heart of financial disasters. For instance, in 2008, the collapse of Lehman Brothers symbolized the failure of regulatory oversight and the systemic vulnerabilities within the global banking system. The repercussions were catastrophic: millions of people lost their jobs, homes, and savings. Central banks had to intervene on a massive scale, implementing quantitative easing and slashing interest rates to stabilize markets. More recently, the COVID-19 pandemic tested the resilience of banks, which, under tighter regulations post-2008, proved more robust. However, new challenges such as inflation, war, and digital disruptions continue to pose threats to economic stability. The global economy has experienced several significant recessions throughout history, many of which were either triggered or exacerbated by the banking sector. From the Great Depression in 1929 to the Global Financial Crisis in 2008, banks have played a pivotal role in shaping the trajectory of economic growth and collapse. Poor regulation, excessive risk-taking, and a lack of transparency have often been at the heart of financial disasters. For instance, in 2008, the collapse of Lehman Brothers symbolized the failure of regulatory oversight and the systemic vulnerabilities within the global banking system. The repercussions were catastrophic: millions of people lost their jobs, homes, and savings. Central banks had to intervene on a massive scale, implementing quantitative easing and slashing interest rates to stabilize markets. More recently, the COVID-19 pandemic tested the resilience of banks, which, under tighter regulations post-2008, proved more robust. However, new challenges such as inflation, war, and digital disruptions continue to pose threats to economic stability. The global economy has experienced several significant recessions throughout history, many of which were either triggered or exacerbated by the banking sector. From the Great Depression in 1929 to the Global Financial Crisis in 2008, banks have played a pivotal role in shaping the trajectory of economic growth and collapse. Poor regulation, excessive risk-taking, and a lack of transparency have often been at the heart of financial disasters. For instance, in 2008, the collapse of Lehman Brothers symbolized the failure of regulatory oversight and the systemic vulnerabilities within the global banking system. The repercussions were catastrophic: millions of people lost their jobs, homes, and savings. Central banks had to intervene on a massive scale, implementing quantitative easing and slashing interest rates to stabilize markets. More recently, the COVID-19 pandemic tested the resilience of banks, which, under tighter regulations post-2008, proved more robust. However, new challenges such as inflation, war, and digital disruptions continue to pose threats to economic stability. The global economy has experienced several significant recessions throughout history, many of which were either triggered or exacerbated by the banking sector. From the Great Depression in 1929 to the Global Financial Crisis in 2008, banks have played a pivotal role in shaping the trajectory of economic growth and collapse. Poor regulation, excessive risk-taking, and a lack of transparency have often been at the heart of financial disasters. For instance, in 2008, the collapse of Lehman Brothers symbolized the failure of regulatory oversight and the systemic vulnerabilities within the global banking system. The repercussions were catastrophic: millions of people lost their jobs, homes, and savings. Central banks had to intervene on a massive scale, implementing quantitative easing and slashing interest rates to stabilize markets. More recently, the COVID-19 pandemic tested the resilience of banks, which, under tighter regulations post-2008, proved more robust. However, new challenges such as inflation, war, and digital disruptions continue to pose threats to economic stability. The global economy has experienced several significant recessions throughout history, many of which were either triggered or exacerbated by the banking sector. From the Great Depression in 1929 to the Global Financial Crisis in 2008, banks have played a pivotal role in shaping the trajectory of economic growth and collapse. Poor regulation, excessive risk-taking, and a lack of transparency have often been at the heart of financial disasters. For instance, in 2008, the collapse of Lehman Brothers symbolized the failure of regulatory oversight and the systemic vulnerabilities within the global banking system. The repercussions were catastrophic: millions of people lost their jobs, homes, and savings. Central banks had to intervene on a massive scale, implementing quantitative easing and slashing interest rates to stabilize markets. More recently, the COVID-19 pandemic tested the resilience of banks, which, under tighter regulations post-2008, proved more robust. However, new challenges such as inflation, war, and digital disruptions continue to pose threats to economic stability. The global economy has experienced several significant recessions throughout history, many of which were either triggered or exacerbated by the banking sector. From the Great Depression in 1929 to the Global Financial Crisis in 2008, banks have played a pivotal role in shaping the trajectory of economic growth and collapse. Poor regulation, excessive risk-taking, and a lack of transparency have often been at the heart of financial disasters. For instance, in 2008, the collapse of Lehman Brothers symbolized the failure of regulatory oversight and the systemic vulnerabilities within the global banking system. The repercussions were catastrophic: millions of people lost their jobs, homes, and savings. Central banks had to intervene on a massive scale, implementing quantitative easing and slashing interest rates to stabilize markets. More recently, the COVID-19 pandemic tested the resilience of banks, which, under tighter regulations post-2008, proved more robust. However, new challenges such as inflation, war, and digital disruptions continue to pose threats to economic stability. The global economy has experienced several significant recessions throughout history, many of which were either triggered or exacerbated by the banking sector. From the Great Depression in 1929 to the Global Financial Crisis in 2008, banks have played a pivotal role in shaping the trajectory of economic growth and collapse. Poor regulation, excessive risk-taking, and a lack of transparency have often been at the heart of financial disasters. For instance, in 2008, the collapse of Lehman Brothers symbolized the failure of regulatory oversight and the systemic vulnerabilities within the global banking system. The repercussions were catastrophic: millions of people lost their jobs, homes, and savings. Central banks had to intervene on a massive scale, implementing quantitative easing and slashing interest rates to stabilize markets. More recently, the COVID-19 pandemic tested the resilience of banks, which, under tighter regulations post-2008, proved more robust. However, new challenges such as inflation, war, and digital disruptions continue to pose threats to economic stability. The global economy has experienced several significant recessions throughout history, many of which were either triggered or exacerbated by the banking sector. From the Great Depression in 1929 to the Global Financial Crisis in 2008, banks have played a pivotal role in shaping the trajectory of economic growth and collapse. Poor regulation, excessive risk-taking, and a lack of transparency have often been at the heart of financial disasters. For instance, in 2008, the collapse of Lehman Brothers symbolized the failure of regulatory oversight and the systemic vulnerabilities within the global banking system. The repercussions were catastrophic: millions of people lost their jobs, homes, and savings. Central banks had to intervene on a massive scale, implementing quantitative easing and slashing interest rates to stabilize markets. More recently, the COVID-19 pandemic tested the resilience of banks, which, under tighter regulations post-2008, proved more robust. However, new challenges such as inflation, war, and digital disruptions continue to pose threats to economic stability. The global economy has experienced several significant recessions throughout history, many of which were either triggered or exacerbated by the banking sector. From the Great Depression in 1929 to the Global Financial Crisis in 2008, banks have played a pivotal role in shaping the trajectory of economic growth and collapse. Poor regulation, excessive risk-taking, and a lack of transparency have often been at the heart of financial disasters. For instance, in 2008, the collapse of Lehman Brothers symbolized the failure of regulatory oversight and the systemic vulnerabilities within the global banking system. The repercussions were catastrophic: millions of people lost their jobs, homes, and savings. Central banks had to intervene on a massive scale, implementing quantitative easing and slashing interest rates to stabilize markets. More recently, the COVID-19 pandemic tested the resilience of banks, which, under tighter regulations post-2008, proved more robust. However, new challenges such as inflation, war, and digital disruptions continue to pose threats to economic stability. The global economy has experienced several significant recessions throughout history, many of which were either triggered or exacerbated by the banking sector. From the Great Depression in 1929 to the Global Financial Crisis in 2008, banks have played a pivotal role in shaping the trajectory of economic growth and collapse. Poor regulation, excessive risk-taking, and a lack of transparency have often been at the heart of financial disasters. For instance, in

2008, the collapse of Lehman Brothers symbolized the failure of regulatory oversight and the systemic vulnerabilities within the global banking system. The repercussions were catastrophic: millions of people lost their jobs, homes, and savings. Central banks had to intervene on a massive scale, implementing quantitative easing and slashing interest rates to stabilize markets. More recently, the COVID-19 pandemic tested the resilience of banks, which, under tighter regulations post-2008, proved more robust. However, new challenges such as inflation, war, and digital disruptions continue to pose threats to economic stability. The global economy has experienced several significant recessions throughout history, many of which were either triggered or exacerbated by the banking sector. From the Great Depression in 1929 to the Global Financial Crisis in 2008, banks have played a pivotal role in shaping the trajectory of economic growth and collapse. Poor regulation, excessive risk-taking, and a lack of transparency have often been at the heart of financial disasters. For instance, in 2008, the collapse of Lehman Brothers symbolized the failure of regulatory oversight and the systemic vulnerabilities within the global banking system. The repercussions were catastrophic: millions of people lost their jobs, homes, and savings. Central banks had to intervene on a massive scale, implementing quantitative easing and slashing interest rates to stabilize markets. More recently, the COVID-19 pandemic tested the resilience of banks, which, under tighter regulations post-2008, proved more robust. However, new challenges such as inflation, war, and digital disruptions continue to pose threats to economic stability. The global economy has experienced several significant recessions throughout history, many of which were either triggered or exacerbated by the banking sector. From the Great Depression in 1929 to the Global Financial Crisis in 2008, banks have played a pivotal role in shaping the trajectory of economic growth and collapse. Poor regulation, excessive risk-taking, and a lack of transparency have often been at the heart of financial disasters. For instance, in 2008, the collapse of Lehman Brothers symbolized the failure of regulatory oversight and the systemic vulnerabilities within the global banking system. The repercussions were catastrophic: millions of people lost their jobs, homes, and savings. Central banks had to intervene on a massive scale, implementing quantitative easing and slashing interest rates to stabilize markets. More recently, the COVID-19 pandemic tested the resilience of banks, which, under tighter regulations post-2008, proved more robust. However, new challenges such as inflation, war, and digital disruptions continue to pose threats to economic stability. The global economy has experienced several significant recessions throughout history, many of which were either triggered or exacerbated by the banking sector. From the Great Depression in 1929 to the Global Financial Crisis in 2008, banks have played a pivotal role in shaping the trajectory of economic growth and collapse. Poor regulation, excessive risk-taking, and a lack of transparency have often been at the heart of financial disasters. For instance, in 2008, the collapse of Lehman Brothers symbolized the failure of regulatory oversight and the systemic vulnerabilities within the global banking system. The repercussions were catastrophic: millions of people lost their jobs, homes, and savings. Central banks had to intervene on a massive scale, implementing quantitative easing and slashing interest rates to stabilize markets. More recently, the COVID-19 pandemic tested the resilience of banks, which, under tighter regulations post-2008, proved more robust. However, new challenges such as inflation, war, and digital disruptions continue to pose threats to economic stability. The global economy has experienced several significant recessions throughout history, many of which were either triggered or exacerbated by the banking sector. From the Great Depression in 1929 to the Global Financial Crisis in 2008, banks have played a pivotal role in shaping the trajectory of economic growth and collapse. Poor regulation, excessive risk-taking, and a lack of transparency have often been at the heart of financial disasters. For instance, in 2008, the collapse of Lehman Brothers symbolized the failure of regulatory oversight and the systemic vulnerabilities within the global banking system. The repercussions were catastrophic: millions of people lost their jobs, homes, and savings. Central banks had to intervene on a massive scale, implementing quantitative easing and slashing interest rates to stabilize markets. More recently, the COVID-19 pandemic tested the resilience of banks, which, under tighter regulations post-2008, proved more robust. However, new challenges such as inflation, war, and digital disruptions continue to pose threats to economic stability. The global economy has experienced several significant recessions throughout history, many of which were either triggered or exacerbated by the banking sector. From the Great Depression in 1929 to the Global Financial Crisis in 2008, banks have played a pivotal role in shaping the trajectory of economic growth and collapse. Poor regulation, excessive risk-taking, and a lack of transparency have often been at the heart of financial disasters. For instance, in 2008, the collapse of Lehman Brothers symbolized the failure of regulatory oversight and the systemic vulnerabilities within the global banking system. The repercussions were catastrophic: millions of people lost their jobs, homes, and savings. Central banks had to intervene on a massive scale, implementing quantitative easing and slashing interest rates to stabilize markets. More recently, the COVID-19 pandemic tested the resilience of banks, which, under tighter regulations post-2008, proved more robust. However, new challenges such as inflation, war, and digital disruptions continue to pose threats to economic stability. The global economy has experienced several significant recessions throughout history, many of which were either triggered or exacerbated by the banking sector. From the Great Depression in 1929 to the Global Financial Crisis in 2008, banks have played a pivotal role in shaping the trajectory of economic growth and collapse. Poor regulation, excessive risk-taking, and a lack of transparency have often been at the heart of financial disasters. For instance, in 2008, the collapse of Lehman Brothers symbolized the failure of regulatory oversight and the systemic vulnerabilities within the global banking system. The repercussions were catastrophic: millions of people lost their jobs, homes, and savings. Central banks had to intervene on a massive scale, implementing quantitative easing and slashing interest rates to stabilize markets. More recently, the COVID-19 pandemic tested the resilience of banks, which, under tighter regulations post-2008, proved more robust. However, new challenges such as inflation, war, and digital disruptions continue to pose threats to economic stability. The global economy has experienced several significant recessions throughout history, many of which were either triggered or exacerbated by the banking sector. From the Great Depression in 1929 to the Global Financial Crisis in 2008, banks have played a pivotal role in shaping the trajectory of economic growth and collapse. Poor regulation, excessive risk-taking, and a lack of transparency have often been at the heart of financial disasters. For instance, in 2008, the collapse of Lehman Brothers symbolized the failure of regulatory oversight and the systemic vulnerabilities within the global banking system. The repercussions were catastrophic: millions of people lost their jobs, homes, and savings. Central banks had to intervene on a massive scale, implementing quantitative easing and slashing interest rates to stabilize markets. More recently, the COVID-19 pandemic tested the resilience of banks, which, under tighter regulations post-2008, proved more robust. However, new challenges such as inflation, war, and digital disruptions continue to pose threats to economic stability. The global economy has experienced several significant recessions throughout history, many of which were either triggered or exacerbated by the banking sector. From the Great Depression in 1929 to the Global Financial Crisis in 2008, banks have played a pivotal role in shaping the trajectory of economic growth and collapse. Poor regulation, excessive risk-taking, and a lack of transparency have often been at the heart of financial disasters. For instance, in 2008, the collapse of Lehman Brothers symbolized the failure of regulatory oversight and the systemic vulnerabilities within the global banking system. The repercussions were catastrophic: millions of people lost their jobs, homes, and savings. Central banks had to intervene on a massive scale, implementing quantitative easing and slashing interest rates to stabilize markets. More recently, the COVID-19 pandemic tested the resilience of banks, which, under tighter regulations post-2008, proved more robust. However, new challenges such as inflation, war, and digital disruptions continue to pose threats to economic stability. The global economy has experienced several significant recessions throughout history, many of which were either triggered or exacerbated by the banking sector. From the Great Depression in 1929 to the Global Financial Crisis in 2008, banks have played a pivotal role in shaping the trajectory of economic growth and collapse. Poor regulation, excessive risk-taking, and a lack of transparency have often been at the heart of financial disasters. For instance, in 2008, the collapse of Lehman Brothers symbolized the failure of regulatory oversight and the systemic vulnerabilities within the global banking system. The repercussions were catastrophic: millions of people lost their jobs, homes, and savings. Central banks had to intervene on a massive scale, implementing quantitative easing and slashing interest rates to stabilize markets. More recently, the COVID-19 pandemic tested the resilience of banks, which, under tighter regulations post-2008, proved more robust. However, new challenges such as inflation, war, and digital disruptions continue to pose threats to economic stability. The global economy has experienced several significant recessions throughout history, many of which were either triggered or exacerbated by the banking sector. From the Great Depression in 1929 to the Global Financial Crisis in 2008, banks have played a pivotal role in shaping the trajectory of economic growth and collapse. Poor regulation, excessive risk-taking, and a lack of transparency have often been at the heart of financial disasters. For instance, in 2008, the collapse of Lehman Brothers symbolized the failure of regulatory oversight and the systemic vulnerabilities within the global banking system. The repercussions were catastrophic: millions of people lost their jobs, homes, and savings. Central banks had to intervene on a massive scale, implementing quantitative easing and slashing interest rates to stabilize markets. More recently, the COVID-19 pandemic tested the resilience of banks, which, under tighter regulations post-2008, proved more robust. However, new challenges such as inflation, war, and digital disruptions continue to pose threats to economic stability. The global economy has experienced several significant recessions throughout history, many of which were either triggered or exacerbated by the banking sector. From the Great Depression in 1929 to the Global Financial Crisis in 2008, banks have played a pivotal role in shaping the trajectory of economic growth and collapse. Poor regulation, excessive risk-taking, and a lack of transparency have often been at the heart of financial disasters. For instance, in 2008, the collapse of Lehman Brothers symbolized the failure of regulatory oversight and the systemic vulnerabilities within the global banking system. The repercussions were catastrophic: millions of people lost their jobs, homes, and savings. Central banks had to intervene on a massive scale, implementing quantitative easing and slashing interest rates to stabilize markets. More recently, the COVID-19 pandemic tested the resilience of banks, which, under tighter regulations post-2008, proved more robust. However, new challenges such as inflation, war, and digital disruptions continue to pose threats to economic stability. The global economy has experienced several significant recessions throughout history, many of which were either triggered or exacerbated by the banking sector. From the Great Depression in 1929 to the Global Financial Crisis in 2008, banks have played a pivotal role in shaping the trajectory of economic growth and collapse. Poor regulation, excessive risk-taking, and a lack of transparency have often been at the heart of financial disasters. For instance, in 2008, the collapse of Lehman Brothers symbolized the failure of regulatory oversight and the systemic vulnerabilities within the global banking system. The repercussions were catastrophic: millions of people lost their jobs, homes, and savings. Central banks had to intervene on a massive scale, implementing quantitative easing and slashing interest rates to stabilize markets. More recently, the COVID-19 pandemic tested the resilience of banks, which, under tighter regulations post-2008, proved more robust. However, new challenges such as inflation, war, and digital disruptions continue to pose threats to economic stability. The global economy has experienced several significant recessions throughout history, many of which were either triggered or exacerbated by the banking sector. From the Great Depression in 1929 to the Global Financial Crisis in 2008, banks have played a pivotal role in shaping the trajectory of economic growth and collapse. Poor regulation, excessive risk-taking, and a lack of transparency have often been at the heart of financial disasters. For instance, in 2008, the collapse of Lehman Brothers symbolized the failure of regulatory oversight and the systemic vulnerabilities within the global banking system. The repercussions were catastrophic: millions of people lost their jobs, homes, and savings. Central banks had to intervene on a massive scale, implementing quantitative easing and slashing interest rates to stabilize markets. More recently, the COVID-19 pandemic tested the resilience of banks, which, under tighter regulations post-2008, proved more robust. However, new challenges such as inflation, war, and digital disruptions continue to pose threats to economic stability. The global economy has experienced several significant recessions throughout history, many of which were either triggered or exacerbated by the banking sector. From the Great Depression in 1929 to the Global Financial Crisis in 2008, banks have played a pivotal role in shaping the trajectory of economic growth and collapse. Poor regulation, excessive risk-taking, and a lack of transparency have often been at the heart of financial disasters. For instance, in 2008, the collapse of Lehman Brothers symbolized the failure of regulatory oversight and the systemic vulnerabilities within the global banking system. The repercussions were catastrophic: millions of people lost their jobs, homes, and savings. Central banks had to intervene on a massive scale, implementing quantitative easing and slashing interest rates to stabilize markets. More recently, the COVID-19 pandemic tested the resilience of banks, which, under tighter regulations post-2008, proved more robust. However, new challenges such as inflation, war, and digital disruptions continue to pose threats to economic stability. The global economy has experienced several significant recessions throughout history, many of which were either triggered or exacerbated by the banking sector. From the Great Depression in 1929 to the Global Financial Crisis in 2008, banks have played a pivotal role in shaping the trajectory of economic growth and collapse. Poor regulation, excessive risk-taking, and a lack of transparency have often been at the heart of financial disasters. For instance, in 2008, the collapse of Lehman Brothers symbolized the failure of regulatory oversight and the systemic vulnerabilities within the global banking system. The repercussions were catastrophic: millions of people lost their jobs, homes, and savings. Central banks had to intervene on a massive scale, implementing quantitative easing and slashing interest rates to stabilize markets. More recently, the COVID-19 pandemic tested the resilience of banks, which, under tighter regulations post-2008, proved more robust. However, new challenges such as inflation, war, and digital disruptions continue to pose threats to economic stability. The global economy has experienced several significant recessions throughout history, many of which were either triggered or exacerbated by the banking sector. From the Great

Depression in 1929 to the Global Financial Crisis in 2008, banks have played a pivotal role in shaping the trajectory of economic growth and collapse. Poor regulation, excessive risk-taking, and a lack of transparency have often been at the heart of financial disasters. For instance, in 2008, the collapse of Lehman Brothers symbolized the failure of regulatory oversight and the systemic vulnerabilities within the global banking system. The repercussions were catastrophic: millions of people lost their jobs, homes, and savings. Central banks had to intervene on a massive scale, implementing quantitative easing and slashing interest rates to stabilize markets. More recently, the COVID-19 pandemic tested the resilience of banks, which, under tighter regulations post-2008, proved more robust. However, new challenges such as inflation, war, and digital disruptions continue to pose threats to economic stability. The global economy has experienced several significant recessions throughout history, many of which were either triggered or exacerbated by the banking sector. From the Great Depression in 1929 to the Global Financial Crisis in 2008, banks have played a pivotal role in shaping the trajectory of economic growth and collapse. Poor regulation, excessive risk-taking, and a lack of transparency have often been at the heart of financial disasters. For instance, in 2008, the collapse of Lehman Brothers symbolized the failure of regulatory oversight and the systemic vulnerabilities within the global banking system. The repercussions were catastrophic: millions of people lost their jobs, homes, and savings. Central banks had to intervene on a massive scale, implementing quantitative easing and slashing interest rates to stabilize markets. More recently, the COVID-19 pandemic tested the resilience of banks, which, under tighter regulations post-2008, proved more robust. However, new challenges such as inflation, war, and digital disruptions continue to pose threats to economic stability. The global economy has experienced several significant recessions throughout history, many of which were either triggered or exacerbated by the banking sector. From the Great Depression in 1929 to the Global Financial Crisis in 2008, banks have played a pivotal role in shaping the trajectory of economic growth and collapse. Poor regulation, excessive risk-taking, and a lack of transparency have often been at the heart of financial disasters. For instance, in 2008, the collapse of Lehman Brothers symbolized the failure of regulatory oversight and the systemic vulnerabilities within the global banking system. The repercussions were catastrophic: millions of people lost their jobs, homes, and savings. Central banks had to intervene on a massive scale, implementing quantitative easing and slashing interest rates to stabilize markets. More recently, the COVID-19 pandemic tested the resilience of banks, which, under tighter regulations post-2008, proved more robust. However, new challenges such as inflation, war, and digital disruptions continue to pose threats to economic stability. The global economy has experienced several significant recessions throughout history, many of which were either triggered or exacerbated by the banking sector. From the Great Depression in 1929 to the Global Financial Crisis in 2008, banks have played a pivotal role in shaping the trajectory of economic growth and collapse. Poor regulation, excessive risk-taking, and a lack of transparency have often been at the heart of financial disasters. For instance, in 2008, the collapse of Lehman Brothers symbolized the failure of regulatory oversight and the systemic vulnerabilities within the global banking system. The repercussions were catastrophic:

millions of people lost their jobs, homes, and savings. Central banks had to intervene on a massive scale, implementing quantitative easing and slashing interest rates to stabilize markets. More recently, the COVID-19 pandemic tested the resilience of banks, which, under tighter regulations post-2008, proved more robust. However, new challenges such as inflation, war, and digital disruptions continue to pose threats to economic stability. The global economy has experienced several significant recessions throughout history, many of which were either triggered or exacerbated by the banking sector. From the Great Depression in 1929 to the Global Financial Crisis in 2008, banks have played a pivotal role in shaping the trajectory of economic growth and collapse. Poor regulation, excessive risk-taking, and a lack of transparency have often been at the heart of financial disasters. For instance, in 2008, the collapse of Lehman Brothers symbolized the failure of regulatory oversight and the systemic vulnerabilities within the global banking system. The repercussions were catastrophic: millions of people lost their jobs, homes, and savings. Central banks had to intervene on a massive scale, implementing quantitative easing and slashing interest rates to stabilize markets. More recently, the COVID-19 pandemic tested the resilience of banks, which, under tighter regulations post-2008, proved more robust. However, new challenges such as inflation, war, and digital disruptions continue to pose threats to economic stability. The global economy has experienced several significant recessions throughout history, many of which were either triggered or exacerbated by the banking sector. From the Great Depression in 1929 to the Global Financial Crisis in 2008, banks have played a pivotal role in shaping the trajectory of economic growth and collapse. Poor regulation, excessive risk-taking, and a lack of transparency have often been at the heart of financial disasters. For instance, in 2008, the collapse of Lehman Brothers symbolized the failure of regulatory oversight and the systemic vulnerabilities within the global banking system. The repercussions were catastrophic: millions of people lost their jobs, homes, and savings. Central banks had to intervene on a massive scale, implementing quantitative easing and slashing interest rates to stabilize markets. More recently, the COVID-19 pandemic tested the resilience of banks, which, under tighter regulations post-2008, proved more robust. However, new challenges such as inflation, war, and digital disruptions continue to pose threats to economic stability. The global economy has experienced several significant recessions throughout history, many of which were either triggered or exacerbated by the banking sector. From the Great Depression in 1929 to the Global Financial Crisis in 2008, banks have played a pivotal role in shaping the trajectory of economic growth and collapse. Poor regulation, excessive risk-taking, and a lack of transparency have often been at the heart of financial disasters. For instance, in 2008, the collapse of Lehman Brothers symbolized the failure of regulatory oversight and the systemic vulnerabilities within the global banking system. The repercussions were catastrophic: millions of people lost their jobs, homes, and savings. Central banks had to intervene on a massive scale, implementing quantitative easing and slashing interest rates to stabilize markets. More recently, the COVID-19 pandemic tested the resilience of banks, which, under tighter regulations post-2008, proved more robust. However, new challenges such as inflation, war, and digital disruptions continue to pose threats to economic stability. The global economy has experienced several significant recessions throughout history, many of which were either triggered or exacerbated by the banking sector. From the Great Depression in 1929 to the Global Financial Crisis in 2008, banks have played a pivotal role in shaping the trajectory of economic growth and collapse. Poor regulation, excessive risk-taking, and a lack of transparency have often been at the heart of financial disasters. For instance, in 2008, the collapse of Lehman Brothers symbolized the failure of regulatory oversight and the systemic vulnerabilities within the global banking system. The repercussions were catastrophic: millions of people lost their jobs, homes, and savings. Central banks had to intervene on a massive scale, implementing quantitative easing and slashing interest rates to stabilize markets. More recently, the COVID-19 pandemic tested the resilience of banks, which, under tighter regulations post-2008, proved more robust. However, new challenges such as inflation, war, and digital disruptions continue to pose threats to economic stability. The global economy has experienced several significant recessions throughout history, many of which were either triggered or exacerbated by the banking sector. From the Great Depression in 1929 to the Global Financial Crisis in 2008, banks have played a pivotal role in shaping the trajectory of economic growth and collapse. Poor regulation, excessive risk-taking, and a lack of transparency have often been at the heart of financial disasters. For instance, in 2008, the collapse of Lehman Brothers symbolized the failure of regulatory oversight and the systemic vulnerabilities within the global banking system. The repercussions were catastrophic: millions of people lost their jobs, homes, and savings. Central banks had to intervene on a massive scale, implementing quantitative easing and slashing interest rates to stabilize markets. More recently, the COVID-19 pandemic tested the resilience of banks, which, under tighter regulations post-2008, proved more robust. However, new challenges such as inflation, war, and digital disruptions continue to pose threats to economic stability. The global economy has experienced several significant recessions throughout history, many of which were either triggered or exacerbated by the banking sector. From the Great Depression in 1929 to the Global Financial Crisis in 2008, banks have played a pivotal role in shaping the trajectory of economic growth and collapse. Poor regulation, excessive risk-taking, and a lack of transparency have often been at the heart of financial disasters. For instance, in 2008, the collapse of Lehman Brothers symbolized the failure of regulatory oversight and the systemic vulnerabilities within the global banking system. The repercussions were catastrophic: millions of people lost their jobs, homes, and savings. Central banks had to intervene on a massive scale, implementing quantitative easing and slashing interest rates to stabilize markets. More recently, the COVID-19 pandemic tested the resilience of banks, which, under tighter regulations post-2008, proved more robust. However, new challenges such as inflation, war, and digital disruptions continue to pose threats to economic stability. The global economy has experienced several significant recessions throughout history, many of which were either triggered or exacerbated by the banking sector. From the Great Depression in 1929 to the Global Financial Crisis in 2008, banks have played a pivotal role in shaping the trajectory of economic growth and collapse. Poor regulation, excessive risk-taking, and a lack of transparency have often been at the heart of financial disasters. For instance, in 2008, the collapse of Lehman Brothers symbolized the failure of regulatory oversight and the systemic vulnerabilities within the global banking system. The repercussions were catastrophic: millions of people lost their jobs, homes, and savings. Central banks had to intervene on a massive scale, implementing quantitative easing and slashing interest rates to stabilize markets. More recently, the COVID-19 pandemic tested the resilience of banks, which, under tighter regulations post-2008, proved more robust. However, new challenges such as inflation, war, and digital disruptions continue to pose threats to economic stability. The global economy has experienced several significant recessions throughout history, many of which were either triggered or exacerbated by the banking sector. From the Great Depression in 1929 to the Global Financial Crisis in 2008, banks have played a pivotal role in shaping the trajectory of economic growth and collapse. Poor regulation, excessive risk-taking, and a lack of transparency have often been at the heart of financial disasters. For instance, in 2008, the collapse of Lehman Brothers symbolized the failure of regulatory oversight and the systemic vulnerabilities within the global banking system. The repercussions were catastrophic: millions of people lost their jobs, homes, and savings. Central banks had to intervene on a massive scale, implementing quantitative easing and slashing interest rates to stabilize markets. More recently, the COVID-19 pandemic tested the resilience of banks, which, under tighter regulations post-2008, proved more robust. However, new challenges such as inflation, war, and digital disruptions continue to pose threats to economic stability. The global economy has experienced several significant recessions throughout history, many of which were either triggered or exacerbated by the banking sector. From the Great Depression in 1929 to the Global Financial Crisis in 2008, banks have played a pivotal role in shaping the trajectory of economic growth and collapse. Poor regulation, excessive risk-taking, and a lack of transparency have often been at the heart of financial disasters. For instance, in 2008, the collapse of Lehman Brothers symbolized the failure of regulatory oversight and the systemic vulnerabilities within the global banking system. The repercussions were catastrophic: millions of people lost their jobs, homes, and savings. Central banks had to intervene on a massive scale, implementing quantitative easing and slashing interest rates to stabilize markets. More recently, the COVID-19 pandemic tested the resilience of banks, which, under tighter regulations post-2008, proved more robust. However, new challenges such as inflation, war, and digital disruptions continue to pose threats to economic stability. The global economy has experienced several significant recessions throughout history, many of which were either triggered or exacerbated by the banking sector. From the Great Depression in 1929 to the Global Financial Crisis in 2008, banks have played a pivotal role in shaping the trajectory of economic growth and collapse. Poor regulation, excessive risk-taking, and a lack of transparency have often been at the heart of financial disasters. For instance, in 2008, the collapse of Lehman Brothers symbolized the failure of regulatory oversight and the systemic vulnerabilities within the global banking system. The repercussions were catastrophic: millions of people lost their jobs, homes, and savings. Central banks had to intervene on a massive scale, implementing quantitative easing and slashing interest rates to stabilize markets. More recently, the COVID-19 pandemic tested the resilience of banks, which, under tighter regulations post-2008, proved more robust. However, new challenges such as inflation, war, and digital disruptions continue to pose threats to economic stability. The global economy has experienced several significant recessions throughout history, many of which were either triggered or exacerbated by the banking sector. From the Great Depression in 1929 to the Global Financial Crisis in 2008, banks have played a pivotal role in shaping the trajectory of economic growth and collapse. Poor regulation, excessive risk-taking, and a lack of transparency have often been at the heart of financial disasters. For instance, in 2008, the collapse of Lehman Brothers symbolized the failure of regulatory oversight and the systemic vulnerabilities within the global banking system. The repercussions were catastrophic: millions of people lost their jobs, homes, and savings. Central banks had to intervene on a massive scale, implementing quantitative easing and slashing interest rates to stabilize markets. More recently, the COVID-19 pandemic tested the resilience of banks, which, under tighter regulations post-2008, proved more robust. However, new challenges such as inflation, war, and digital disruptions continue to pose threats to economic stability. The global economy has experienced several significant recessions throughout history, many of which were either triggered or exacerbated by the banking sector. From the Great Depression in 1929 to the Global Financial Crisis in 2008, banks have played a pivotal role in shaping the trajectory of economic growth and collapse. Poor regulation, excessive risk-taking, and a lack of transparency have often been at the heart of financial disasters. For instance, in 2008, the collapse of Lehman Brothers symbolized the failure of regulatory oversight and the systemic vulnerabilities within the global banking system. The repercussions were catastrophic: millions of people lost their jobs, homes, and savings. Central banks had to intervene on a massive scale, implementing quantitative easing and slashing interest rates to stabilize markets. More recently, the COVID-19 pandemic tested the resilience of banks, which, under tighter regulations post-2008, proved more robust. However, new challenges such as inflation, war, and digital disruptions continue to pose threats to economic stability. The global economy has experienced several significant recessions throughout history, many of which were either triggered or exacerbated by the banking sector. From the Great Depression in 1929 to the Global Financial Crisis in 2008, banks have played a pivotal role in shaping the trajectory of economic growth and collapse. Poor regulation, excessive risk-taking, and a lack of transparency have often been at the heart of financial disasters. For instance, in 2008, the collapse of Lehman Brothers symbolized the failure of regulatory oversight and the systemic vulnerabilities within the global banking system. The repercussions were catastrophic: millions of people lost their jobs, homes, and savings. Central banks had to intervene on a massive scale, implementing quantitative easing and slashing interest rates to stabilize markets. More recently, the COVID-19 pandemic tested the resilience of banks, which, under tighter regulations post-2008, proved more robust. However, new challenges such as inflation, war, and digital disruptions continue to pose threats to economic stability. The global economy has experienced several significant recessions throughout history, many of which were either triggered or exacerbated by the banking sector. From the Great Depression in 1929 to the Global Financial Crisis in 2008, banks have played a pivotal role in shaping the trajectory of economic growth and collapse. Poor regulation, excessive risk-taking, and a lack of transparency have often been at the heart of financial disasters. For instance, in 2008, the collapse of Lehman Brothers symbolized the failure of regulatory oversight and the systemic vulnerabilities within the global banking system. The repercussions were catastrophic: millions of people lost their jobs, homes, and savings. Central banks had to intervene on a massive scale, implementing quantitative easing and slashing interest rates to stabilize markets. More recently, the COVID-19 pandemic tested the resilience of banks, which, under tighter regulations post-2008, proved more robust. However, new challenges such as inflation, war, and digital disruptions continue to pose threats to economic stability. The global economy has experienced several significant recessions throughout history, many of which were either triggered or exacerbated by the banking sector. From the Great Depression in 1929 to the Global Financial Crisis in 2008, banks have played a pivotal role in shaping the trajectory of economic growth and collapse. Poor regulation, excessive risk-taking, and a lack of transparency have often been at the heart of financial disasters. For instance, in 2008, the collapse of Lehman Brothers symbolized the failure of regulatory oversight and the systemic vulnerabilities within the global banking system. The repercussions were catastrophic: millions of people lost their jobs, homes, and savings. Central banks had to intervene on a massive scale, implementing quantitative easing and slashing interest rates to stabilize markets. More recently, the COVID-19 pandemic tested the resilience of banks, which, under tighter regulations post-2008, proved more robust. However, new challenges such as inflation, war, and digital disruptions continue to pose threats to economic stability. The global economy has experienced several significant recessions throughout history, many of which were either triggered or exacerbated by the banking sector. From the Great Depression in 1929 to the Global Financial Crisis in 2008, banks have played a pivotal role in shaping the trajectory of economic growth and collapse. Poor regulation, excessive risk-taking, and a lack of transparency have often been at the heart of financial disasters. For instance, in 2008, the collapse of Lehman Brothers symbolized the failure of regulatory oversight and the systemic vulnerabilities within the global banking system. The repercussions were catastrophic: millions of people lost their jobs, homes, and savings. Central banks had to intervene on a massive scale, implementing quantitative easing and slashing interest rates to stabilize markets. More recently, the COVID-19 pandemic tested the resilience of banks, which, under tighter regulations post-2008, proved more robust. However, new challenges such as inflation, war, and digital disruptions continue to pose threats to economic stability. The global economy has experienced several significant recessions throughout history, many of which were either triggered or exacerbated by the banking sector. From the Great Depression in 1929 to the Global Financial Crisis in 2008, banks have played a pivotal role in shaping the trajectory of economic growth and collapse. Poor regulation, excessive risk-taking, and a lack of transparency have often been at the heart of financial disasters. For instance, in 2008, the collapse of Lehman Brothers symbolized the failure of regulatory oversight and the systemic vulnerabilities within the global banking system. The repercussions were catastrophic: millions of people lost their jobs, homes, and savings. Central banks had to intervene on a massive scale, implementing quantitative easing and slashing interest rates to stabilize markets. More recently, the COVID-19 pandemic tested the resilience of banks, which, under tighter regulations post-2008, proved more robust. However, new challenges such as inflation, war, and digital disruptions continue to pose threats to economic stability. The global economy has experienced several significant recessions throughout history, many of which were either triggered or exacerbated by the banking sector. From the Great Depression in 1929 to the Global Financial Crisis in 2008, banks have played a pivotal role in shaping the trajectory of economic growth and collapse. Poor regulation, excessive risk-taking, and a lack of transparency have often been at the heart of financial disasters. For instance, in 2008, the collapse of Lehman Brothers symbolized the failure of regulatory oversight and the systemic vulnerabilities within the global banking system. The repercussions were catastrophic: millions of people lost their jobs, homes, and savings. Central banks had to intervene on a massive scale, implementing quantitative easing and slashing interest rates to stabilize markets. More recently, the COVID-19 pandemic tested the resilience of banks, which, under tighter regulations post-2008, proved more robust. However, new challenges such as inflation, war, and digital disruptions continue to pose threats to economic stability. The global economy has experienced several significant recessions throughout history, many of which were either triggered or exacerbated by the banking sector. From the Great Depression in 1929 to the Global Financial Crisis in 2008, banks have played a pivotal role in shaping the trajectory of economic growth and collapse. Poor regulation, excessive risk-taking, and a lack of transparency have often been at the heart of financial disasters. For instance, in 2008, the collapse of Lehman Brothers symbolized the failure of regulatory oversight and the systemic vulnerabilities within the global banking system. The repercussions were catastrophic: millions of people lost their jobs, homes, and savings. Central banks had to intervene on a massive scale, implementing quantitative easing and slashing interest rates to stabilize markets.

More recently, the COVID-19 pandemic tested the resilience of banks, which, under tighter regulations post-2008, proved more robust. However, new challenges such as inflation, war, and digital disruptions continue to pose threats to economic stability. The global economy has experienced several significant recessions throughout history, many of which were either triggered or exacerbated by the banking sector. From the Great Depression in 1929 to the Global Financial Crisis in 2008, banks have played a pivotal role in shaping the trajectory of economic growth and collapse. Poor regulation, excessive risk-taking, and a lack of transparency have often been at the heart of financial disasters. For instance, in 2008, the collapse of Lehman Brothers symbolized the failure of regulatory oversight and the systemic vulnerabilities within the global banking system. The repercussions were catastrophic: millions of people lost their jobs, homes, and savings. Central banks had to intervene on a massive scale, implementing quantitative easing and slashing interest rates to stabilize markets. More recently, the COVID-19 pandemic tested the resilience of banks, which, under tighter regulations post-2008, proved more robust. However, new challenges such as inflation, war, and digital disruptions continue to pose threats to economic stability. The global economy has experienced several significant recessions throughout history, many of which were either triggered or exacerbated by the banking sector. From the Great Depression in 1929 to the Global Financial Crisis in 2008, banks have played a pivotal role in shaping the trajectory of economic growth and collapse. Poor regulation, excessive risk-taking, and a lack of transparency have often been at the heart of financial disasters. For instance, in 2008, the collapse of Lehman Brothers symbolized the failure of regulatory oversight and the systemic vulnerabilities within the global banking system. The repercussions were catastrophic: millions of people lost their jobs, homes, and savings. Central banks had to intervene on a massive scale, implementing quantitative easing and slashing interest rates to stabilize markets. More recently, the COVID-19 pandemic tested the resilience of banks, which, under tighter regulations post-2008, proved more robust. However, new challenges such as inflation, war, and digital disruptions continue to pose threats to economic stability. The global economy has experienced several significant recessions throughout history, many of which were either triggered or exacerbated by the banking sector. From the Great Depression in 1929 to the Global Financial Crisis in 2008, banks have played a pivotal role in shaping the trajectory of economic growth and collapse. Poor regulation, excessive risk-taking, and a lack of transparency have often been at the heart of financial disasters. For instance, in 2008, the collapse of Lehman Brothers symbolized the failure of regulatory oversight and the systemic vulnerabilities within the global banking system. The repercussions were catastrophic: millions of people lost their jobs, homes, and savings. Central banks had to intervene on a massive scale, implementing quantitative easing and slashing interest rates to stabilize markets. More recently, the COVID-19 pandemic tested the resilience of banks, which, under tighter regulations post-2008, proved more robust. However, new challenges such as inflation, war, and digital disruptions continue to pose threats to economic stability. The global economy has experienced several significant recessions throughout history, many of which were either triggered or exacerbated by the banking sector. From the Great Depression in 1929 to the Global

Financial Crisis in 2008, banks have played a pivotal role in shaping the trajectory of economic growth and collapse. Poor regulation, excessive risk-taking, and a lack of transparency have often been at the heart of financial disasters. For instance, in 2008, the collapse of Lehman Brothers symbolized the failure of regulatory oversight and the systemic vulnerabilities within the global banking system. The repercussions were catastrophic: millions of people lost their jobs, homes, and savings. Central banks had to intervene on a massive scale, implementing quantitative easing and slashing interest rates to stabilize markets. More recently, the COVID-19 pandemic tested the resilience of banks, which, under tighter regulations post-2008, proved more robust. However, new challenges such as inflation, war, and digital disruptions continue to pose threats to economic stability. The global economy has experienced several significant recessions throughout history, many of which were either triggered or exacerbated by the banking sector. From the Great Depression in 1929 to the Global Financial Crisis in 2008, banks have played a pivotal role in shaping the trajectory of economic growth and collapse. Poor regulation, excessive risk-taking, and a lack of transparency have often been at the heart of financial disasters. For instance, in 2008, the collapse of Lehman Brothers symbolized the failure of regulatory oversight and the systemic vulnerabilities within the global banking system. The repercussions were catastrophic: millions of people lost their jobs, homes, and savings. Central banks had to intervene on a massive scale, implementing quantitative easing and slashing interest rates to stabilize markets. More recently, the COVID-19 pandemic tested the resilience of banks, which, under tighter regulations post-2008, proved more robust. However, new challenges such as inflation, war, and digital disruptions continue to pose threats to economic stability. The global economy has experienced several significant recessions throughout history, many of which were either triggered or exacerbated by the banking sector. From the Great Depression in 1929 to the Global Financial Crisis in 2008, banks have played a pivotal role in shaping the trajectory of economic growth and collapse. Poor regulation, excessive risk-taking, and a lack of transparency have often been at the heart of financial disasters. For instance, in 2008, the collapse of Lehman Brothers symbolized the failure of regulatory oversight and the systemic vulnerabilities within the global banking system. The repercussions were catastrophic: millions of people lost their jobs, homes, and savings. Central banks had to intervene on a massive scale, implementing quantitative easing and slashing interest rates to stabilize markets. More recently, the COVID-19 pandemic tested the resilience of banks, which, under tighter regulations post-2008, proved more robust. However, new challenges such as inflation, war, and digital disruptions continue to pose threats to economic stability. The global economy has experienced several significant recessions throughout history, many of which were either triggered or exacerbated by the banking sector. From the Great Depression in 1929 to the Global Financial Crisis in 2008, banks have played a pivotal role in shaping the trajectory of economic growth and collapse. Poor regulation, excessive risk-taking, and a lack of transparency have often been at the heart of financial disasters. For instance, in 2008, the collapse of Lehman Brothers symbolized the failure of regulatory oversight and the systemic vulnerabilities within the global banking system. The repercussions were catastrophic: millions of people lost their jobs, homes, and savings. Central banks had to intervene on a massive scale, implementing quantitative easing and slashing interest rates to stabilize markets. More recently, the COVID-19 pandemic tested the resilience of banks, which, under tighter regulations post-2008, proved more robust. However, new challenges such as inflation, war, and digital disruptions continue to pose threats to economic stability. The global economy has experienced several significant recessions throughout history, many of which were either triggered or exacerbated by the banking sector. From the Great Depression in 1929 to the Global Financial Crisis in 2008, banks have played a pivotal role in shaping the trajectory of economic growth and collapse. Poor regulation, excessive risk-taking, and a lack of transparency have often been at the heart of financial disasters. For instance, in 2008, the collapse of Lehman Brothers symbolized the failure of regulatory oversight and the systemic vulnerabilities within the global banking system. The repercussions were catastrophic: millions of people lost their jobs, homes, and savings. Central banks had to intervene on a massive scale, implementing quantitative easing and slashing interest rates to stabilize markets. More recently, the COVID-19 pandemic tested the resilience of banks, which, under tighter regulations post-2008, proved more robust. However, new challenges such as inflation, war, and digital disruptions continue to pose threats to economic stability. The global economy has experienced several significant recessions throughout history, many of which were either triggered or exacerbated by the banking sector. From the Great Depression in 1929 to the Global Financial Crisis in 2008, banks have played a pivotal role in shaping the trajectory of economic growth and collapse. Poor regulation, excessive risk-taking, and a lack of transparency have often been at the heart of financial disasters. For instance, in 2008, the collapse of Lehman Brothers symbolized the failure of regulatory oversight and the systemic vulnerabilities within the global banking system. The repercussions were catastrophic: millions of people lost their jobs, homes, and savings. Central banks had to intervene on a massive scale, implementing quantitative easing and slashing interest rates to stabilize markets. More recently, the COVID-19 pandemic tested the resilience of banks, which, under tighter regulations post-2008, proved more robust. However, new challenges such as inflation, war, and digital disruptions continue to pose threats to economic stability. The global economy has experienced several significant recessions throughout history, many of which were either triggered or exacerbated by the banking sector. From the Great Depression in 1929 to the Global Financial Crisis in 2008, banks have played a pivotal role in shaping the trajectory of economic growth and collapse. Poor regulation, excessive risk-taking, and a lack of transparency have often been at the heart of financial disasters. For instance, in 2008, the collapse of Lehman Brothers symbolized the failure of regulatory oversight and the systemic vulnerabilities within the global banking system. The repercussions were catastrophic: millions of people lost their jobs, homes, and savings. Central banks had to intervene on a massive scale, implementing quantitative easing and slashing interest rates to stabilize markets. More recently, the COVID-19 pandemic tested the resilience of banks, which, under tighter regulations post-2008, proved more robust. However, new challenges such as inflation, war, and digital disruptions continue to pose threats to economic stability. The global economy has experienced several significant recessions throughout history, many of which were either triggered or exacerbated by the banking sector. From the Great Depression in 1929 to the Global Financial Crisis in 2008, banks have played a pivotal role in shaping the trajectory of economic growth and collapse. Poor regulation, excessive risk-taking, and a lack of transparency have often been at the heart of financial disasters. For instance, in 2008, the collapse of Lehman Brothers symbolized the failure of regulatory oversight and the systemic vulnerabilities within the global banking system. The repercussions were catastrophic: millions of people lost their jobs, homes, and savings. Central banks had to intervene on a massive scale, implementing quantitative easing and slashing interest rates to stabilize markets. More recently, the COVID-19 pandemic tested the resilience of banks, which, under tighter regulations post-2008, proved more robust. However, new challenges such as inflation, war, and digital disruptions continue to pose threats to economic stability. The global economy has experienced several significant recessions throughout history, many of which were either triggered or exacerbated by the banking sector. From the Great Depression in 1929 to the Global Financial Crisis in 2008, banks have played a pivotal role in shaping the trajectory of economic growth and collapse. Poor regulation, excessive risk-taking, and a lack of transparency have often been at the heart of financial disasters. For instance, in 2008, the collapse of Lehman Brothers symbolized the failure of regulatory oversight and the systemic vulnerabilities within the global banking system. The repercussions were catastrophic: millions of people lost their jobs, homes, and savings. Central banks had to intervene on a massive scale, implementing quantitative easing and slashing interest rates to stabilize markets. More recently, the COVID-19 pandemic tested the resilience of banks, which, under tighter regulations post-2008, proved more robust. However, new challenges such as inflation, war, and digital disruptions continue to pose threats to economic stability. The global economy has experienced several significant recessions throughout history, many of which were either triggered or exacerbated by the banking sector. From the Great Depression in 1929 to the Global Financial Crisis in 2008, banks have played a pivotal role in shaping the trajectory of economic growth and collapse. Poor regulation, excessive risk-taking, and a lack of transparency have often been at the heart of financial disasters. For instance, in 2008, the collapse of Lehman Brothers symbolized the failure of regulatory oversight and the systemic vulnerabilities within the global banking system. The repercussions were catastrophic: millions of people lost their jobs, homes, and savings. Central banks had to intervene on a massive scale, implementing quantitative easing and slashing interest rates to stabilize markets. More recently, the COVID-19 pandemic tested the resilience of banks, which, under tighter regulations post-2008, proved more robust. However, new challenges such as inflation, war, and digital disruptions continue to pose threats to economic stability. The global economy has experienced several significant recessions throughout history, many of which were either triggered or exacerbated by the banking sector. From the Great Depression in 1929 to the Global Financial Crisis in 2008, banks have played a pivotal role in shaping the trajectory of economic growth and collapse. Poor regulation, excessive risk-taking, and a lack of transparency have often been at the heart of financial disasters. For instance, in 2008, the collapse of Lehman Brothers symbolized the failure of regulatory oversight and the systemic vulnerabilities within the global banking system. The repercussions were catastrophic: millions of people lost their jobs, homes, and savings. Central banks had to intervene on a massive scale, implementing quantitative easing and slashing interest rates to stabilize markets. More recently, the COVID-19 pandemic tested the resilience of banks, which, under tighter regulations post-2008, proved more robust. However, new challenges such as inflation, war, and digital disruptions continue to pose threats to economic stability. The global economy has experienced several significant recessions throughout history, many of which were either triggered or exacerbated by the banking sector. From the Great Depression in 1929 to the Global Financial Crisis in 2008, banks have played a pivotal role in shaping the trajectory of economic growth and collapse. Poor regulation, excessive risk-taking, and a lack of transparency have often been at the heart of financial disasters. For instance, in 2008, the collapse of Lehman Brothers symbolized the failure of regulatory oversight and the systemic vulnerabilities within the global banking system. The repercussions were catastrophic: millions of people lost their jobs, homes, and savings. Central banks had to intervene on a massive scale, implementing quantitative easing and slashing interest rates to stabilize markets. More recently, the COVID-19 pandemic tested the resilience of banks, which, under tighter regulations post-2008, proved more robust. However, new challenges such as inflation, war, and digital disruptions continue to pose threats to economic stability. The global economy has experienced several significant recessions throughout history, many of which were either triggered or exacerbated by the banking sector. From the Great Depression in 1929 to the Global Financial Crisis in 2008, banks have played a pivotal role in shaping the trajectory of economic growth and collapse. Poor regulation, excessive risk-taking, and a lack of transparency have often been at the heart of financial disasters. For instance, in 2008, the collapse of Lehman Brothers symbolized the failure of regulatory oversight and the systemic vulnerabilities within the global banking system. The repercussions were catastrophic: millions of people lost their jobs, homes, and savings. Central banks had to intervene on a massive scale, implementing quantitative easing and slashing interest rates to stabilize markets. More recently, the COVID-19 pandemic tested the resilience of banks, which, under tighter regulations post-2008, proved more robust. However, new challenges such as inflation, war, and digital disruptions continue to pose threats to economic stability. The global economy has experienced several significant recessions throughout history, many of which were either triggered or exacerbated by the banking sector. From the Great Depression in 1929 to the Global Financial Crisis in 2008, banks have played a pivotal role in shaping the trajectory of economic growth and collapse. Poor regulation, excessive risk-taking, and a lack of transparency have often been at the heart of financial disasters. For instance, in 2008, the collapse of Lehman Brothers symbolized the failure of regulatory oversight and the systemic vulnerabilities within the global banking system. The repercussions were catastrophic: millions of people lost their jobs, homes, and savings. Central banks had to intervene on a massive scale, implementing quantitative easing and slashing interest rates to stabilize markets. More recently, the COVID-19 pandemic tested the resilience of banks, which, under tighter regulations post-2008, proved more robust. However, new challenges such as inflation, war, and digital disruptions continue to pose threats to economic stability. The global economy has experienced several significant recessions throughout history, many of which were either triggered or exacerbated by the banking sector. From the Great Depression in 1929 to the Global Financial Crisis in 2008, banks have played a pivotal role in shaping the trajectory of economic growth and collapse. Poor regulation, excessive risk-taking, and a lack of transparency have often been at the heart of financial disasters. For instance, in 2008, the collapse of Lehman Brothers symbolized the failure of regulatory oversight and the systemic vulnerabilities within the global banking system. The repercussions were catastrophic: millions of people lost their jobs, homes, and savings. Central banks had to intervene on a massive scale, implementing quantitative easing and slashing interest rates to stabilize markets. More recently, the COVID-19 pandemic tested the resilience of banks, which, under tighter regulations post-2008, proved more robust. However, new challenges such as inflation, war, and digital disruptions continue to pose threats to economic stability. The global economy has experienced several significant recessions throughout history, many of which were either triggered or exacerbated by the banking sector. From the Great Depression in 1929 to the Global Financial Crisis in 2008, banks have played a pivotal role in shaping the trajectory of economic growth and collapse. Poor regulation, excessive risk-taking, and a lack of transparency have often been at the heart of financial disasters. For instance, in 2008, the collapse of Lehman Brothers symbolized the failure of regulatory oversight and the systemic vulnerabilities within the global banking system. The repercussions were catastrophic: millions of people lost their jobs, homes, and savings. Central banks had to intervene on a massive scale, implementing quantitative easing and slashing interest rates to stabilize markets. More recently, the COVID-19 pandemic tested the resilience of banks, which, under tighter regulations post-2008, proved more robust. However, new challenges such as inflation, war, and digital disruptions continue to pose threats to economic stability. The global economy has experienced several significant recessions throughout history, many of which were either triggered or exacerbated by the banking sector. From the Great Depression in 1929 to the Global Financial Crisis in 2008, banks have played a pivotal role in shaping the trajectory of economic growth and collapse. Poor regulation, excessive risk-taking, and a lack of transparency have often been at the heart of financial disasters. For instance, in 2008, the collapse of Lehman Brothers symbolized the failure of regulatory oversight and the systemic vulnerabilities within the global banking system. The repercussions were catastrophic: millions of people lost their jobs, homes, and savings. Central banks had to intervene on a massive scale, implementing quantitative easing and slashing interest rates to stabilize markets. More recently, the COVID-19 pandemic tested the resilience of banks, which, under tighter regulations post-2008, proved more robust. However, new challenges such as inflation, war, and digital disruptions continue to pose threats to economic stability. The global economy has experienced several significant recessions throughout history, many of which were either triggered or exacerbated by the banking sector. From the Great Depression in 1929 to the Global Financial Crisis in 2008, banks have played a pivotal role in shaping the trajectory of economic growth and collapse. Poor regulation, excessive risk-taking, and a lack of transparency have often been at the heart of financial disasters. For instance, in 2008, the collapse of Lehman Brothers symbolized the failure of regulatory oversight and the systemic vulnerabilities within the global banking system. The repercussions were catastrophic: millions of people lost their jobs, homes, and savings. Central banks had to intervene on a massive scale, implementing quantitative easing and slashing interest rates to stabilize markets. More recently, the COVID-19 pandemic tested the resilience of banks, which, under tighter regulations post-2008, proved more robust. However, new challenges such as inflation, war, and digital disruptions continue to pose threats to economic stability. The global economy has experienced several significant recessions throughout history, many of which were either triggered or exacerbated by the banking sector. From the Great Depression in 1929 to the Global Financial Crisis in 2008, banks have played a pivotal role in shaping the trajectory of economic growth and collapse. Poor regulation, excessive risk-taking, and a lack of transparency have often been at the heart of financial disasters. For instance, in 2008, the collapse of Lehman Brothers symbolized the failure of regulatory oversight and the systemic vulnerabilities within the global banking system. The repercussions were catastrophic: millions of people lost their jobs, homes, and savings. Central banks had to intervene on a massive scale, implementing quantitative easing and slashing interest rates to stabilize markets. More recently, the COVID-19 pandemic tested the resilience of banks, which, under tighter regulations post-2008, proved more robust. However, new challenges such as inflation, war, and digital disruptions continue to pose threats to economic stability. The global economy has experienced several significant recessions throughout history, many of which were either triggered or exacerbated by the banking sector. From the Great Depression in 1929 to the Global Financial Crisis in 2008, banks have played a pivotal role in shaping the trajectory of economic growth and collapse. Poor regulation, excessive risk-taking, and a lack of transparency have often been at the heart of financial disasters. For instance, in 2008, the collapse of Lehman Brothers symbolized the failure of regulatory oversight and the systemic vulnerabilities within the global banking system. The repercussions were catastrophic: millions of people lost their jobs, homes, and savings. Central banks had to intervene on a massive scale, implementing quantitative easing and slashing interest rates to stabilize markets. More recently, the COVID-19 pandemic tested the resilience of banks, which, under tighter regulations post-2008, proved more robust. However, new challenges such as inflation, war, and digital disruptions continue to pose threats to economic stability. The global economy has experienced several significant recessions throughout history, many of which were either triggered or exacerbated by the banking sector. From the Great Depression in 1929 to the Global Financial Crisis in 2008, banks have played a pivotal role in shaping the trajectory of economic growth and collapse. Poor regulation, excessive risk-taking, and a lack of transparency have often been at the heart of financial disasters. For instance, in 2008, the collapse of Lehman Brothers symbolized the failure of regulatory oversight and the systemic vulnerabilities within the global banking system. The repercussions were catastrophic: millions of people lost their jobs, homes, and savings. Central banks had to intervene on a massive scale, implementing quantitative easing and slashing interest rates to stabilize markets. More recently, the COVID-19 pandemic tested the resilience of banks, which, under tighter regulations post-2008, proved more robust. However, new challenges such as inflation, war, and digital disruptions continue to pose threats to economic stability. The global economy has experienced several significant recessions throughout history, many of which were either triggered or exacerbated by the banking sector. From the Great Depression in 1929 to the Global Financial Crisis in 2008, banks have played a pivotal role in shaping the trajectory of economic growth and collapse. Poor regulation, excessive risk-taking, and a lack of transparency have often been at the heart of financial disasters. For instance, in 2008, the collapse of Lehman Brothers symbolized the failure of regulatory oversight and the systemic vulnerabilities within the global banking system. The repercussions were catastrophic: millions of people lost their jobs, homes, and savings. Central banks had to intervene on a massive scale, implementing quantitative easing and slashing interest rates to stabilize markets. More recently, the COVID-19 pandemic tested the resilience of banks, which, under tighter regulations post-2008, proved more robust. However, new challenges such as inflation, war, and digital disruptions continue to pose threats to economic stability. The global economy has experienced several significant recessions throughout history, many of which were either triggered or exacerbated by the banking sector. From the Great Depression in 1929 to the Global Financial Crisis in 2008, banks have played a pivotal role in shaping the trajectory of economic growth and collapse. Poor regulation, excessive risk-taking, and a lack of transparency have often been at the heart of financial disasters. For instance, in 2008, the collapse of Lehman Brothers symbolized the failure of regulatory oversight and the systemic vulnerabilities within the global banking system. The repercussions were catastrophic: millions of people lost their jobs, homes, and savings. Central banks had to intervene on a massive scale, implementing quantitative easing and slashing interest rates to stabilize markets. More recently, the COVID-19 pandemic tested the resilience of banks, which, under tighter regulations post-2008, proved more robust. However, new challenges such as inflation, war, and digital disruptions continue to pose threats to economic stability. The global economy has experienced several significant recessions throughout history, many of which were either triggered or exacerbated by the banking sector. From the Great Depression in 1929 to the Global Financial Crisis in 2008, banks have played a pivotal role in shaping the trajectory of economic growth and collapse. Poor regulation, excessive risk-taking, and a lack of transparency have often been at the heart of financial disasters. For instance, in 2008, the collapse of Lehman Brothers symbolized the failure of regulatory oversight and the systemic vulnerabilities within the global banking system. The repercussions were catastrophic: millions of people lost their jobs, homes, and savings. Central banks had to intervene on a massive scale, implementing quantitative easing and slashing interest rates to stabilize markets. More recently, the COVID-19 pandemic tested the resilience of banks, which, under tighter regulations post-2008, proved more robust. However, new challenges such as inflation, war, and digital disruptions continue to pose threats to economic stability. The global economy has experienced several significant recessions throughout history, many of which were either triggered or exacerbated by the banking sector. From the Great Depression in 1929 to the Global Financial Crisis in 2008, banks have played a pivotal role in shaping the trajectory of economic growth and collapse. Poor regulation, excessive risk-taking, and a lack of transparency have often been at the heart of financial disasters. For instance, in 2008, the collapse of Lehman Brothers symbolized the failure of regulatory oversight and the systemic vulnerabilities within the global banking system. The repercussions were catastrophic: millions of people lost their jobs, homes, and savings. Central banks had to intervene on a massive scale, implementing quantitative easing and slashing interest rates to stabilize markets. More recently, the COVID-19 pandemic tested the resilience of banks, which, under tighter regulations post-2008, proved more robust. However, new challenges such as inflation, war, and digital disruptions continue to pose threats to economic stability. The global economy has experienced several significant recessions throughout history, many of which were either triggered or exacerbated by the banking sector. From the Great Depression in 1929 to the Global Financial Crisis in 2008, banks have played a pivotal role in shaping the trajectory of economic growth and collapse. Poor regulation, excessive risk-taking, and a lack of transparency have often been at the heart of financial disasters. For instance, in 2008, the collapse of Lehman Brothers symbolized the failure of regulatory oversight and the systemic vulnerabilities within the global banking system. The repercussions were catastrophic: millions of people lost their jobs, homes, and savings. Central banks had to intervene on a massive scale, implementing quantitative easing and slashing interest rates to stabilize markets. More recently, the COVID-19 pandemic tested the resilience of banks, which, under tighter regulations post-2008, proved more robust. However, new challenges such as inflation, war, and digital disruptions continue to pose threats to economic stability. The global economy has experienced several significant recessions throughout history, many of which were either triggered or exacerbated by the banking sector. From the Great Depression in 1929 to the Global Financial Crisis in 2008, banks have played a pivotal role in shaping the trajectory of economic growth and collapse. Poor regulation, excessive risk-taking, and a lack of transparency have often been at the heart of financial disasters. For instance, in 2008, the collapse of Lehman Brothers symbolized the failure of regulatory oversight and the systemic vulnerabilities within the global banking system. The repercussions were catastrophic: millions of people lost their jobs, homes, and savings. Central banks had to intervene on a massive scale, implementing quantitative easing and slashing interest rates to stabilize markets. More recently, the COVID-19 pandemic tested the resilience of banks, which, under tighter regulations post-2008, proved more robust. However, new challenges such as inflation, war, and digital disruptions continue to pose threats to economic stability. The global economy has experienced several significant recessions throughout history, many of which were either triggered or exacerbated by the banking sector. From the Great Depression in 1929 to the Global Financial Crisis in 2008, banks have played a pivotal role in shaping the trajectory of economic growth and collapse. Poor regulation, excessive risk-taking, and a lack of transparency have often been at the heart of financial disasters. For instance, in 2008, the collapse of Lehman Brothers symbolized the failure of regulatory oversight and the systemic vulnerabilities within the global banking system. The repercussions were catastrophic: millions of people lost their jobs, homes, and savings. Central banks had to intervene on a massive scale, implementing quantitative easing and slashing interest rates to stabilize markets. More recently, the COVID-19 pandemic tested the resilience of banks, which, under tighter regulations post-2008, proved more robust. However, new challenges such as inflation, war, and digital disruptions continue to pose threats to economic stability. The global economy has experienced several significant recessions throughout history, many of which were either triggered or exacerbated by the banking sector. From the Great Depression in 1929 to the Global Financial Crisis in 2008, banks have played a pivotal role in shaping the trajectory of economic growth and collapse. Poor regulation, excessive risk-taking, and a lack of transparency have often been at the heart of financial disasters. For instance, in 2008, the collapse of Lehman Brothers symbolized the failure of regulatory oversight and the systemic vulnerabilities within the global banking system. The repercussions were catastrophic: millions of people lost their jobs, homes, and savings. Central banks had to intervene on a massive scale, implementing quantitative easing and slashing interest rates to stabilize markets. More recently, the COVID-19 pandemic tested the resilience of banks, which, under tighter regulations post-2008, proved more robust. However, new challenges such as inflation, war, and digital disruptions continue to pose threats to economic stability. The global economy has experienced several significant recessions throughout history, many of which were either triggered or exacerbated by the banking sector. From the Great Depression in 1929 to the Global Financial Crisis in 2008, banks have played a pivotal role in shaping the trajectory of economic growth and collapse. Poor regulation, excessive risk-taking, and a lack of transparency have often been at the heart of financial disasters. For instance, in 2008, the collapse of Lehman Brothers symbolized the failure of regulatory oversight and the systemic vulnerabilities within the global banking system. The repercussions were catastrophic: millions of people lost their jobs, homes, and savings. Central banks had to intervene on a massive scale, implementing quantitative easing and slashing interest rates to stabilize markets. More recently, the COVID-19 pandemic tested the resilience of banks, which, under tighter regulations post-2008, proved more robust. However, new challenges such as inflation, war, and digital disruptions continue to pose threats to economic stability. The global economy has experienced several significant recessions throughout history, many of which were either triggered or exacerbated by the banking sector. From the Great Depression in 1929 to the Global Financial Crisis in 2008, banks have played a pivotal role in shaping the trajectory of economic growth and collapse. Poor regulation, excessive risk-taking, and a lack of transparency have often been at the heart of financial disasters. For instance, in 2008, the collapse of Lehman Brothers symbolized the failure of regulatory oversight and the systemic vulnerabilities within the global banking system. The repercussions were catastrophic: millions of people lost their jobs, homes, and savings. Central banks had to intervene on a massive scale, implementing quantitative easing and slashing interest rates to stabilize markets. More recently, the COVID-19 pandemic tested the resilience of banks, which, under tighter regulations post-2008, proved more robust. However, new challenges such as inflation, war, and digital disruptions continue to pose threats to economic stability. The global economy has experienced several significant recessions throughout history, many of which were either triggered or exacerbated by the banking sector. From the Great Depression in 1929 to the Global Financial Crisis in 2008, banks have played a pivotal role in shaping the trajectory of economic growth and collapse. Poor regulation, excessive risk-taking, and a lack of transparency have often been at the heart of financial disasters. For instance, in 2008, the collapse of Lehman Brothers symbolized the failure of regulatory oversight and the systemic vulnerabilities within the global banking system. The repercussions were catastrophic: millions of people lost their jobs, homes, and savings. Central banks had to intervene on a massive scale, implementing quantitative easing and slashing interest rates to stabilize markets. More recently, the COVID-19 pandemic tested the resilience of banks, which, under tighter regulations post-2008, proved more robust. However, new challenges such as inflation, war, and digital disruptions continue to pose threats to economic stability. The global economy has experienced several significant recessions throughout history, many of which were either triggered or exacerbated by the banking sector. From the Great Depression in 1929 to the Global Financial Crisis in 2008, banks have played a pivotal role in shaping the trajectory of economic growth and collapse. Poor regulation, excessive risk-taking, and a lack of transparency have often been at the heart of financial disasters. For instance, in 2008, the collapse of Lehman Brothers symbolized the failure of regulatory oversight and the systemic vulnerabilities within the global banking system. The repercussions were catastrophic: millions of people lost their jobs, homes, and savings. Central banks had to intervene on a massive scale, implementing quantitative easing and slashing interest rates to stabilize markets. More recently, the COVID-19 pandemic tested the resilience of banks, which, under tighter regulations post-2008, proved more robust. However, new challenges such as inflation, war, and digital disruptions continue to pose threats to economic stability. The global economy has experienced several significant recessions throughout history, many of which were either triggered or exacerbated by the banking sector. From the Great Depression in 1929 to the Global Financial Crisis in 2008, banks have played a pivotal role in shaping the trajectory of economic growth and collapse. Poor regulation, excessive risk-taking, and a lack of transparency have often been at the heart of financial disasters. For instance, in 2008, the collapse of Lehman Brothers symbolized the failure of regulatory oversight and the systemic vulnerabilities within the global banking system. The repercussions were catastrophic: millions of people lost their jobs, homes, and savings. Central banks had to intervene on a massive scale, implementing quantitative easing and slashing interest rates to stabilize markets. More recently, the COVID-19 pandemic tested the resilience of banks, which, under tighter regulations post-2008, proved more robust. However, new challenges such as inflation, war, and digital disruptions continue to pose threats to economic stability. The global economy has experienced several significant recessions throughout history, many of which were either triggered or exacerbated by the banking sector. From the Great Depression in 1929 to the Global Financial Crisis in 2008, banks have played a pivotal role in shaping the trajectory of economic growth and collapse. Poor regulation, excessive risk-taking, and a lack of transparency have often been at the heart of financial disasters. For instance, in 2008, the collapse of Lehman Brothers symbolized the failure of regulatory oversight and the systemic vulnerabilities within the global banking system. The repercussions were catastrophic: millions of people lost their jobs, homes, and savings. Central banks had to intervene on a massive scale, implementing quantitative easing and slashing interest rates to stabilize markets. More recently, the COVID-19 pandemic tested the resilience of banks, which, under tighter regulations post-2008, proved more robust. However, new challenges such as inflation, war, and digital disruptions continue to pose threats to economic stability. The global economy has experienced several significant recessions throughout history, many of which were either triggered or exacerbated by the banking sector. From the Great Depression in 1929 to the Global Financial Crisis in 2008, banks have played a pivotal role in shaping the trajectory of economic growth and collapse. Poor regulation, excessive risk-taking, and a lack of transparency have often been at the heart of financial disasters. For instance, in 2008, the collapse of Lehman Brothers symbolized the failure of regulatory oversight and the systemic vulnerabilities within the global banking system. The repercussions were catastrophic: millions of people lost their jobs, homes, and savings. Central banks had to intervene on a massive scale, implementing quantitative easing and slashing interest rates to stabilize markets. More recently, the COVID-19 pandemic tested the resilience of banks, which, under tighter regulations post-2008, proved more robust. However, new challenges such as inflation, war, and digital disruptions continue to pose threats to economic stability. The global economy has experienced several significant recessions throughout history, many of which were either triggered or exacerbated by the banking sector. From the Great Depression in 1929 to the Global Financial Crisis in 2008, banks have played a pivotal role in shaping the trajectory of economic growth and collapse. Poor regulation, excessive risk-taking, and a lack of transparency have often been at the heart of financial disasters. For instance, in 2008, the collapse of Lehman Brothers symbolized the failure of regulatory oversight and the systemic vulnerabilities within the global banking system. The repercussions were catastrophic: millions of people lost their jobs, homes, and savings. Central banks had to intervene on a massive scale, implementing quantitative easing and slashing interest rates to stabilize markets. More recently, the COVID-19 pandemic tested the resilience of banks, which, under tighter regulations post-2008, proved more robust. However, new challenges such as inflation, war, and digital disruptions continue to pose threats to economic stability. The global economy has experienced several significant recessions throughout history, many of which were either triggered or exacerbated by the banking sector. From the Great Depression in 1929 to the Global Financial Crisis in 2008, banks have played a pivotal role in shaping the trajectory of economic growth and collapse. Poor regulation, excessive risk-taking, and a lack of transparency have often been at the heart of financial disasters. For instance, in 2008, the collapse of Lehman Brothers symbolized the failure of regulatory oversight and the systemic vulnerabilities within the global banking system. The repercussions were catastrophic: millions of people lost their jobs, homes, and savings. Central banks had to intervene on a massive scale, implementing quantitative easing and slashing interest rates to stabilize markets. More recently, the COVID-19 pandemic tested the resilience of banks, which, under tighter regulations post-2008, proved more robust. However, new challenges such as inflation, war, and digital disruptions continue to pose threats to economic stability. The global economy has experienced several significant recessions throughout history, many of which were either triggered or exacerbated by the banking sector. From the Great Depression in 1929 to the Global Financial Crisis in 2008, banks have played a pivotal role in shaping the trajectory of economic growth and collapse. Poor regulation, excessive risk-taking, and a lack of transparency have often been at the heart of financial disasters. For instance, in 2008, the collapse of Lehman Brothers symbolized the failure of regulatory oversight and the systemic vulnerabilities within the global banking system. The repercussions were catastrophic: millions of people lost their jobs, homes, and savings. Central banks had to intervene on a massive scale, implementing quantitative easing and slashing interest rates to stabilize markets. More recently, the COVID-19 pandemic tested the resilience of banks, which, under tighter regulations post-2008, proved more robust. However, new challenges such as inflation, war, and digital disruptions continue to pose threats to economic stability. The global economy has experienced several significant recessions throughout history, many of which were either triggered or exacerbated by the banking sector. From the Great Depression in 1929 to the Global Financial Crisis in 2008, banks have played a pivotal role in shaping the trajectory of economic growth and collapse. Poor regulation, excessive risk-taking, and a lack of transparency have often been at the heart of financial disasters. For instance, in 2008, the collapse of Lehman Brothers symbolized the failure of regulatory oversight and the systemic vulnerabilities within the global banking system. The repercussions were catastrophic: millions of people lost their jobs, homes, and savings. Central banks had to intervene on a massive scale, implementing quantitative easing and slashing interest rates to stabilize markets. More recently, the COVID-19 pandemic tested the resilience of banks, which, under tighter regulations post-2008, proved more robust. However, new challenges such as inflation, war, and digital disruptions continue to pose threats to economic stability. The global economy has experienced several significant recessions throughout history, many of which were either triggered or exacerbated by the banking sector. From the Great Depression in 1929 to the Global Financial Crisis in 2008, banks have played a pivotal role in shaping the trajectory of economic growth and collapse. Poor regulation, excessive risk-taking, and a lack of transparency have often been at the heart of financial disasters. For instance, in 2008, the collapse of Lehman Brothers symbolized the failure of regulatory oversight and the systemic vulnerabilities within the global banking system. The repercussions were catastrophic: millions of people lost their jobs, homes, and savings. Central banks had to intervene on a massive scale, implementing quantitative easing and slashing interest rates to stabilize markets. More recently, the COVID-19 pandemic tested the resilience of banks, which, under tighter regulations post-2008, proved more robust. However, new challenges such as inflation, war, and digital disruptions continue to pose threats to economic stability. The global economy has experienced several significant recessions throughout history, many of which were either triggered or exacerbated by the banking sector. From the Great Depression in 1929 to the Global Financial Crisis in 2008, banks have played a pivotal role in shaping the trajectory of economic growth and collapse. Poor regulation, excessive risk-taking, and a lack of transparency have often been at the heart of financial disasters. For instance, in 2008, the collapse of Lehman Brothers symbolized the failure of regulatory oversight and the systemic vulnerabilities within the global banking system. The repercussions were catastrophic: millions of people lost their jobs, homes, and savings. Central banks had to intervene on a massive scale, implementing quantitative easing and slashing interest rates to stabilize markets. More recently, the COVID-19 pandemic tested the resilience of banks, which, under tighter regulations post-2008, proved more robust. However, new challenges such as inflation, war, and digital disruptions continue to pose threats to economic stability. The global economy has experienced several significant recessions throughout history, many of which were either triggered or exacerbated by the banking sector. From the Great Depression in 1929 to the Global Financial Crisis in 2008, banks have played a pivotal role in shaping the trajectory of economic growth and collapse. Poor regulation, excessive risk-taking, and a lack of transparency have often been at the heart of financial disasters. For instance, in 2008, the collapse of Lehman Brothers symbolized the failure of regulatory oversight and the systemic vulnerabilities within the global banking system. The repercussions were catastrophic: millions of people lost their jobs, homes, and savings. Central banks had to intervene on a massive scale, implementing quantitative easing and slashing interest rates to stabilize markets. More recently, the COVID-19 pandemic tested the resilience of banks, which, under tighter regulations post-2008, proved more robust. However, new challenges such as inflation, war, and digital disruptions continue to pose threats to economic stability. The global economy has experienced several significant recessions throughout history, many of which were either triggered or exacerbated by the banking sector. From the Great Depression in 1929 to the Global Financial Crisis in 2008, banks have played a pivotal role in shaping the trajectory of economic growth and collapse. Poor regulation, excessive risk-taking, and a lack of transparency have often been at the heart of financial disasters. For instance, in 2008, the collapse of Lehman Brothers symbolized the failure of regulatory oversight and the systemic vulnerabilities within the global banking system. The repercussions were catastrophic: millions of people lost their jobs, homes, and savings. Central banks had to intervene on a massive scale, implementing quantitative easing and slashing interest rates to stabilize markets. More recently, the COVID-19 pandemic tested the resilience of banks, which, under tighter regulations post-2008, proved more robust. However, new challenges such as inflation, war, and digital disruptions continue to pose threats to economic stability. The global economy has experienced several significant recessions throughout history, many of which were either triggered or exacerbated by the banking sector. From the Great Depression in 1929 to the Global Financial Crisis in 2008, banks have played a pivotal role in shaping the trajectory of economic growth and collapse. Poor regulation, excessive risk-taking, and a lack of transparency have often been at the heart of financial disasters. For instance, in 2008, the collapse of Lehman Brothers symbolized the failure of regulatory oversight and the systemic vulnerabilities within the global banking system. The repercussions were catastrophic: millions of people lost their jobs, homes, and savings. Central banks had to intervene on a massive scale, implementing quantitative easing and slashing interest rates to stabilize markets. More recently, the COVID-19 pandemic tested the resilience of banks, which, under tighter regulations post-2008, proved more robust. However, new challenges such as inflation, war, and digital disruptions continue to pose threats to economic stability. The global economy has experienced several significant recessions throughout history, many of which were either triggered or exacerbated by the banking sector. From the Great Depression in 1929 to the Global Financial Crisis in 2008, banks have played a pivotal role in shaping the trajectory of economic growth and collapse. Poor regulation, excessive risk-taking, and a lack of transparency have often been at the heart of financial disasters. For instance, in 2008, the collapse of Lehman Brothers symbolized the failure of regulatory oversight and the systemic vulnerabilities within the global banking system. The repercussions were catastrophic: millions of people lost their jobs, homes, and savings. Central banks had to intervene on a massive scale, implementing quantitative easing and slashing interest rates to stabilize markets. More recently, the COVID-19 pandemic tested the resilience of banks, which, under tighter regulations post-2008, proved more robust. However, new challenges such as inflation, war, and digital disruptions continue to pose threats to economic stability. The global economy has experienced several significant recessions throughout history, many of which were either triggered or exacerbated by the banking sector. From the Great Depression in 1929 to the Global Financial Crisis in 2008, banks have played a pivotal role in shaping the trajectory of economic growth and collapse. Poor regulation, excessive risk-taking, and a lack of transparency have often been at the heart of financial disasters. For instance, in 2008, the collapse of Lehman Brothers symbolized the failure of regulatory oversight and the systemic vulnerabilities within the global banking system. The repercussions were catastrophic: millions of people lost their jobs, homes, and savings. Central banks had to intervene on a massive scale, implementing quantitative easing and slashing interest rates to stabilize markets. More recently, the COVID-19 pandemic tested the resilience of banks, which, under tighter regulations post-2008, proved more robust. However, new challenges such as inflation, war, and digital disruptions continue to pose threats to economic stability. The global economy has experienced several significant recessions throughout history, many of which were either triggered or exacerbated by the banking sector. From the Great Depression in 1929 to the Global Financial Crisis in 2008, banks have played a pivotal role in shaping the trajectory of economic growth and collapse. Poor regulation, excessive risk-taking, and a lack of transparency have often been at the heart of financial disasters. For instance, in 2008, the collapse of Lehman Brothers symbolized the failure of regulatory oversight and the systemic vulnerabilities within the global banking system. The repercussions were catastrophic: millions of people lost their jobs, homes, and savings. Central banks had to intervene on a massive scale, implementing quantitative easing and slashing interest rates to stabilize markets. More recently, the COVID-19 pandemic tested the resilience of banks, which, under tighter regulations post-2008, proved more robust. However, new challenges such as inflation, war, and digital disruptions continue to pose threats to economic stability. The global economy has experienced several significant recessions throughout history, many of which were either triggered or exacerbated by the banking sector. From the Great Depression in 1929 to the Global Financial Crisis in 2008, banks have played a pivotal role in shaping the trajectory of economic growth and collapse. Poor regulation, excessive risk-taking, and a lack of transparency have often been at the heart of financial disasters. For instance, in

2008, the collapse of Lehman Brothers symbolized the failure of regulatory oversight and the systemic vulnerabilities within the global banking system. The repercussions were catastrophic: millions of people lost their jobs, homes, and savings. Central banks had to intervene on a massive scale, implementing quantitative easing and slashing interest rates to stabilize markets. More recently, the COVID-19 pandemic tested the resilience of banks, which, under tighter regulations post-2008, proved more robust. However, new challenges such as inflation, war, and digital disruptions continue to pose threats to economic stability. The global economy has experienced several significant recessions throughout history, many of which were either triggered or exacerbated by the banking sector. From the Great Depression in 1929 to the Global Financial Crisis in 2008, banks have played a pivotal role in shaping the trajectory of economic growth and collapse. Poor regulation, excessive risk-taking, and a lack of transparency have often been at the heart of financial disasters. For instance, in 2008, the collapse of Lehman Brothers symbolized the failure of regulatory oversight and the systemic vulnerabilities within the global banking system. The repercussions were catastrophic: millions of people lost their jobs, homes, and savings. Central banks had to intervene on a massive scale, implementing quantitative easing and slashing interest rates to stabilize markets. More recently, the COVID-19 pandemic tested the resilience of banks, which, under tighter regulations post-2008, proved more robust. However, new challenges such as inflation, war, and digital disruptions continue to pose threats to economic stability. The global economy has experienced several significant recessions throughout history, many of which were either triggered or exacerbated by the banking sector. From the Great Depression in 1929 to the Global Financial Crisis in 2008, banks have played a pivotal role in shaping the trajectory of economic growth and collapse. Poor regulation, excessive risk-taking, and a lack of transparency have often been at the heart of financial disasters. For instance, in 2008, the collapse of Lehman Brothers symbolized the failure of regulatory oversight and the systemic vulnerabilities within the global banking system. The repercussions were catastrophic: millions of people lost their jobs, homes, and savings. Central banks had to intervene on a massive scale, implementing quantitative easing and slashing interest rates to stabilize markets. More recently, the COVID-19 pandemic tested the resilience of banks, which, under tighter regulations post-2008, proved more robust. However, new challenges such as inflation, war, and digital disruptions continue to pose threats to economic stability. The global economy has experienced several significant recessions throughout history, many of which were either triggered or exacerbated by the banking sector. From the Great Depression in 1929 to the Global Financial Crisis in 2008, banks have played a pivotal role in shaping the trajectory of economic growth and collapse. Poor regulation, excessive risk-taking, and a lack of transparency have often been at the heart of financial disasters. For instance, in 2008, the collapse of Lehman Brothers symbolized the failure of regulatory oversight and the systemic vulnerabilities within the global banking system. The repercussions were catastrophic: millions of people lost their jobs, homes, and savings. Central banks had to intervene on a massive scale, implementing quantitative easing and slashing interest rates to stabilize markets. More recently, the COVID-19 pandemic tested the resilience of banks, which, under tighter regulations post-2008, proved more robust. However, new challenges such as inflation, war, and digital disruptions continue to pose threats to economic stability. The global economy has experienced several significant recessions throughout history, many of which were either triggered or exacerbated by the banking sector. From the Great Depression in 1929 to the Global Financial Crisis in 2008, banks have played a pivotal role in shaping the trajectory of economic growth and collapse. Poor regulation, excessive risk-taking, and a lack of transparency have often been at the heart of financial disasters. For instance, in 2008, the collapse of Lehman Brothers symbolized the failure of regulatory oversight and the systemic vulnerabilities within the global banking system. The repercussions were catastrophic: millions of people lost their jobs, homes, and savings. Central banks had to intervene on a massive scale, implementing quantitative easing and slashing interest rates to stabilize markets. More recently, the COVID-19 pandemic tested the resilience of banks, which, under tighter regulations post-2008, proved more robust. However, new challenges such as inflation, war, and digital disruptions continue to pose threats to economic stability. The global economy has experienced several significant recessions throughout history, many of which were either triggered or exacerbated by the banking sector. From the Great Depression in 1929 to the Global Financial Crisis in 2008, banks have played a pivotal role in shaping the trajectory of economic growth and collapse. Poor regulation, excessive risk-taking, and a lack of transparency have often been at the heart of financial disasters. For instance, in 2008, the collapse of Lehman Brothers symbolized the failure of regulatory oversight and the systemic vulnerabilities within the global banking system. The repercussions were catastrophic: millions of people lost their jobs, homes, and savings. Central banks had to intervene on a massive scale, implementing quantitative easing and slashing interest rates to stabilize markets. More recently, the COVID-19 pandemic tested the resilience of banks, which, under tighter regulations post-2008, proved more robust. However, new challenges such as inflation, war, and digital disruptions continue to pose threats to economic stability. The global economy has experienced several significant recessions throughout history, many of which were either triggered or exacerbated by the banking sector. From the Great Depression in 1929 to the Global Financial Crisis in 2008, banks have played a pivotal role in shaping the trajectory of economic growth and collapse. Poor regulation, excessive risk-taking, and a lack of transparency have often been at the heart of financial disasters. For instance, in 2008, the collapse of Lehman Brothers symbolized the failure of regulatory oversight and the systemic vulnerabilities within the global banking system. The repercussions were catastrophic: millions of people lost their jobs, homes, and savings. Central banks had to intervene on a massive scale, implementing quantitative easing and slashing interest rates to stabilize markets. More recently, the COVID-19 pandemic tested the resilience of banks, which, under tighter regulations post-2008, proved more robust. However, new challenges such as inflation, war, and digital disruptions continue to pose threats to economic stability. The global economy has experienced several significant recessions throughout history, many of which were either triggered or exacerbated by the banking sector. From the Great Depression in 1929 to the Global Financial Crisis in 2008, banks have played a pivotal role in shaping the trajectory of economic growth and collapse. Poor regulation, excessive risk-taking, and a lack of transparency have often been at the heart of financial disasters. For instance, in 2008, the collapse of Lehman Brothers symbolized the failure of regulatory oversight and the systemic vulnerabilities within the global banking system. The repercussions were catastrophic: millions of people lost their jobs, homes, and savings. Central banks had to intervene on a massive scale, implementing quantitative easing and slashing interest rates to stabilize markets. More recently, the COVID-19 pandemic tested the resilience of banks, which, under tighter regulations post-2008, proved more robust. However, new challenges such as inflation, war, and digital disruptions continue to pose threats to economic stability. The global economy has experienced several significant recessions throughout history, many of which were either triggered or exacerbated by the banking sector. From the Great Depression in 1929 to the Global Financial Crisis in 2008, banks have played a pivotal role in shaping the trajectory of economic growth and collapse. Poor regulation, excessive risk-taking, and a lack of transparency have often been at the heart of financial disasters. For instance, in 2008, the collapse of Lehman Brothers symbolized the failure of regulatory oversight and the systemic vulnerabilities within the global banking system. The repercussions were catastrophic: millions of people lost their jobs, homes, and savings. Central banks had to intervene on a massive scale, implementing quantitative easing and slashing interest rates to stabilize markets. More recently, the COVID-19 pandemic tested the resilience of banks, which, under tighter regulations post-2008, proved more robust. However, new challenges such as inflation, war, and digital disruptions continue to pose threats to economic stability. The global economy has experienced several significant recessions throughout history, many of which were either triggered or exacerbated by the banking sector. From the Great Depression in 1929 to the Global Financial Crisis in 2008, banks have played a pivotal role in shaping the trajectory of economic growth and collapse. Poor regulation, excessive risk-taking, and a lack of transparency have often been at the heart of financial disasters. For instance, in 2008, the collapse of Lehman Brothers symbolized the failure of regulatory oversight and the systemic vulnerabilities within the global banking system. The repercussions were catastrophic: millions of people lost their jobs, homes, and savings. Central banks had to intervene on a massive scale, implementing quantitative easing and slashing interest rates to stabilize markets. More recently, the COVID-19 pandemic tested the resilience of banks, which, under tighter regulations post-2008, proved more robust. However, new challenges such as inflation, war, and digital disruptions continue to pose threats to economic stability. The global economy has experienced several significant recessions throughout history, many of which were either triggered or exacerbated by the banking sector. From the Great Depression in 1929 to the Global Financial Crisis in 2008, banks have played a pivotal role in shaping the trajectory of economic growth and collapse. Poor regulation, excessive risk-taking, and a lack of transparency have often been at the heart of financial disasters. For instance, in 2008, the collapse of Lehman Brothers symbolized the failure of regulatory oversight and the systemic vulnerabilities within the global banking system. The repercussions were catastrophic: millions of people lost their jobs, homes, and savings. Central banks had to intervene on a massive scale, implementing quantitative easing and slashing interest rates to stabilize markets. More recently, the COVID-19 pandemic tested the resilience of banks, which, under tighter regulations post-2008, proved more robust. However, new challenges such as inflation, war, and digital disruptions continue to pose threats to economic stability. The global economy has experienced several significant recessions throughout history, many of which were either triggered or exacerbated by the banking sector. From the Great Depression in 1929 to the Global Financial Crisis in 2008, banks have played a pivotal role in shaping the trajectory of economic growth and collapse. Poor regulation, excessive risk-taking, and a lack of transparency have often been at the heart of financial disasters. For instance, in 2008, the collapse of Lehman Brothers symbolized the failure of regulatory oversight and the systemic vulnerabilities within the global banking system. The repercussions were catastrophic: millions of people lost their jobs, homes, and savings. Central banks had to intervene on a massive scale, implementing quantitative easing and slashing interest rates to stabilize markets. More recently, the COVID-19 pandemic tested the resilience of banks, which, under tighter regulations post-2008, proved more robust. However, new challenges such as inflation, war, and digital disruptions continue to pose threats to economic stability. The global economy has experienced several significant recessions throughout history, many of which were either triggered or exacerbated by the banking sector. From the Great Depression in 1929 to the Global Financial Crisis in 2008, banks have played a pivotal role in shaping the trajectory of economic growth and collapse. Poor regulation, excessive risk-taking, and a lack of transparency have often been at the heart of financial disasters. For instance, in 2008, the collapse of Lehman Brothers symbolized the failure of regulatory oversight and the systemic vulnerabilities within the global banking system. The repercussions were catastrophic: millions of people lost their jobs, homes, and savings. Central banks had to intervene on a massive scale, implementing quantitative easing and slashing interest rates to stabilize markets. More recently, the COVID-19 pandemic tested the resilience of banks, which, under tighter regulations post-2008, proved more robust. However, new challenges such as inflation, war, and digital disruptions continue to pose threats to economic stability. The global economy has experienced several significant recessions throughout history, many of which were either triggered or exacerbated by the banking sector. From the Great Depression in 1929 to the Global Financial Crisis in 2008, banks have played a pivotal role in shaping the trajectory of economic growth and collapse. Poor regulation, excessive risk-taking, and a lack of transparency have often been at the heart of financial disasters. For instance, in 2008, the collapse of Lehman Brothers symbolized the failure of regulatory oversight and the systemic vulnerabilities within the global banking system. The repercussions were catastrophic: millions of people lost their jobs, homes, and savings. Central banks had to intervene on a massive scale, implementing quantitative easing and slashing interest rates to stabilize markets. More recently, the COVID-19 pandemic tested the resilience of banks, which, under tighter regulations post-2008, proved more robust. However, new challenges such as inflation, war, and digital disruptions continue to pose threats to economic stability. The global economy has experienced several significant recessions throughout history, many of which were either triggered or exacerbated by the banking sector. From the Great Depression in 1929 to the Global Financial Crisis in 2008, banks have played a pivotal role in shaping the trajectory of economic growth and collapse. Poor regulation, excessive risk-taking, and a lack of transparency have often been at the heart of financial disasters. For instance, in 2008, the collapse of Lehman Brothers symbolized the failure of regulatory oversight and the systemic vulnerabilities within the global banking system. The repercussions were catastrophic: millions of people lost their jobs, homes, and savings. Central banks had to intervene on a massive scale, implementing quantitative easing and slashing interest rates to stabilize markets. More recently, the COVID-19 pandemic tested the resilience of banks, which, under tighter regulations post-2008, proved more robust. However, new challenges such as inflation, war, and digital disruptions continue to pose threats to economic stability. The global economy has experienced several significant recessions throughout history, many of which were either triggered or exacerbated by the banking sector. From the Great

Depression in 1929 to the Global Financial Crisis in 2008, banks have played a pivotal role in shaping the trajectory of economic growth and collapse. Poor regulation, excessive risk-taking, and a lack of transparency have often been at the heart of financial disasters. For instance, in 2008, the collapse of Lehman Brothers symbolized the failure of regulatory oversight and the systemic vulnerabilities within the global banking system. The repercussions were catastrophic: millions of people lost their jobs, homes, and savings. Central banks had to intervene on a massive scale, implementing quantitative easing and slashing interest rates to stabilize markets. More recently, the COVID-19 pandemic tested the resilience of banks, which, under tighter regulations post-2008, proved more robust. However, new challenges such as inflation, war, and digital disruptions continue to pose threats to economic stability. The global economy has experienced several significant recessions throughout history, many of which were either triggered or exacerbated by the banking sector. From the Great Depression in 1929 to the Global Financial Crisis in 2008, banks have played a pivotal role in shaping the trajectory of economic growth and collapse. Poor regulation, excessive risk-taking, and a lack of transparency have often been at the heart of financial disasters. For instance, in 2008, the collapse of Lehman Brothers symbolized the failure of regulatory oversight and the systemic vulnerabilities within the global banking system. The repercussions were catastrophic: millions of people lost their jobs, homes, and savings. Central banks had to intervene on a massive scale, implementing quantitative easing and slashing interest rates to stabilize markets. More recently, the COVID-19 pandemic tested the resilience of banks, which, under tighter regulations post-2008, proved more robust. However, new challenges such as inflation, war, and digital disruptions continue to pose threats to economic stability. The global economy has experienced several significant recessions throughout history, many of which were either triggered or exacerbated by the banking sector. From the Great Depression in 1929 to the Global Financial Crisis in 2008, banks have played a pivotal role in shaping the trajectory of economic growth and collapse. Poor regulation, excessive risk-taking, and a lack of transparency have often been at the heart of financial disasters. For instance, in 2008, the collapse of Lehman Brothers symbolized the failure of regulatory oversight and the systemic vulnerabilities within the global banking system. The repercussions were catastrophic: millions of people lost their jobs, homes, and savings. Central banks had to intervene on a massive scale, implementing quantitative easing and slashing interest rates to stabilize markets. More recently, the COVID-19 pandemic tested the resilience of banks, which, under tighter regulations post-2008, proved more robust. However, new challenges such as inflation, war, and digital disruptions continue to pose threats to economic stability. The global economy has experienced several significant recessions throughout history, many of which were either triggered or exacerbated by the banking sector. From the Great Depression in 1929 to the Global Financial Crisis in 2008, banks have played a pivotal role in shaping the trajectory of economic growth and collapse. Poor regulation, excessive risk-taking, and a lack of transparency have often been at the heart of financial disasters. For instance, in 2008, the collapse of Lehman Brothers symbolized the failure of regulatory oversight and the systemic vulnerabilities within the global banking system. The repercussions were catastrophic:

millions of people lost their jobs, homes, and savings. Central banks had to intervene on a massive scale, implementing quantitative easing and slashing interest rates to stabilize markets. More recently, the COVID-19 pandemic tested the resilience of banks, which, under tighter regulations post-2008, proved more robust. However, new challenges such as inflation, war, and digital disruptions continue to pose threats to economic stability. The global economy has experienced several significant recessions throughout history, many of which were either triggered or exacerbated by the banking sector. From the Great Depression in 1929 to the Global Financial Crisis in 2008, banks have played a pivotal role in shaping the trajectory of economic growth and collapse. Poor regulation, excessive risk-taking, and a lack of transparency have often been at the heart of financial disasters. For instance, in 2008, the collapse of Lehman Brothers symbolized the failure of regulatory oversight and the systemic vulnerabilities within the global banking system. The repercussions were catastrophic: millions of people lost their jobs, homes, and savings. Central banks had to intervene on a massive scale, implementing quantitative easing and slashing interest rates to stabilize markets. More recently, the COVID-19 pandemic tested the resilience of banks, which, under tighter regulations post-2008, proved more robust. However, new challenges such as inflation, war, and digital disruptions continue to pose threats to economic stability. The global economy has experienced several significant recessions throughout history, many of which were either triggered or exacerbated by the banking sector. From the Great Depression in 1929 to the Global Financial Crisis in 2008, banks have played a pivotal role in shaping the trajectory of economic growth and collapse. Poor regulation, excessive risk-taking, and a lack of transparency have often been at the heart of financial disasters. For instance, in 2008, the collapse of Lehman Brothers symbolized the failure of regulatory oversight and the systemic vulnerabilities within the global banking system. The repercussions were catastrophic: millions of people lost their jobs, homes, and savings. Central banks had to intervene on a massive scale, implementing quantitative easing and slashing interest rates to stabilize markets. More recently, the COVID-19 pandemic tested the resilience of banks, which, under tighter regulations post-2008, proved more robust. However, new challenges such as inflation, war, and digital disruptions continue to pose threats to economic stability. The global economy has experienced several significant recessions throughout history, many of which were either triggered or exacerbated by the banking sector. From the Great Depression in 1929 to the Global Financial Crisis in 2008, banks have played a pivotal role in shaping the trajectory of economic growth and collapse. Poor regulation, excessive risk-taking, and a lack of transparency have often been at the heart of financial disasters. For instance, in 2008, the collapse of Lehman Brothers symbolized the failure of regulatory oversight and the systemic vulnerabilities within the global banking system. The repercussions were catastrophic: millions of people lost their jobs, homes, and savings. Central banks had to intervene on a massive scale, implementing quantitative easing and slashing interest rates to stabilize markets. More recently, the COVID-19 pandemic tested the resilience of banks, which, under tighter regulations post-2008, proved more robust. However, new challenges such as inflation, war, and digital disruptions continue to pose threats to economic stability. The global economy has experienced several significant recessions throughout history, many of which were either triggered or exacerbated by the banking sector. From the Great Depression in 1929 to the Global Financial Crisis in 2008, banks have played a pivotal role in shaping the trajectory of economic growth and collapse. Poor regulation, excessive risk-taking, and a lack of transparency have often been at the heart of financial disasters. For instance, in 2008, the collapse of Lehman Brothers symbolized the failure of regulatory oversight and the systemic vulnerabilities within the global banking system. The repercussions were catastrophic: millions of people lost their jobs, homes, and savings. Central banks had to intervene on a massive scale, implementing quantitative easing and slashing interest rates to stabilize markets. More recently, the COVID-19 pandemic tested the resilience of banks, which, under tighter regulations post-2008, proved more robust. However, new challenges such as inflation, war, and digital disruptions continue to pose threats to economic stability. The global economy has experienced several significant recessions throughout history, many of which were either triggered or exacerbated by the banking sector. From the Great Depression in 1929 to the Global Financial Crisis in 2008, banks have played a pivotal role in shaping the trajectory of economic growth and collapse. Poor regulation, excessive risk-taking, and a lack of transparency have often been at the heart of financial disasters. For instance, in 2008, the collapse of Lehman Brothers symbolized the failure of regulatory oversight and the systemic vulnerabilities within the global banking system. The repercussions were catastrophic: millions of people lost their jobs, homes, and savings. Central banks had to intervene on a massive scale, implementing quantitative easing and slashing interest rates to stabilize markets. More recently, the COVID-19 pandemic tested the resilience of banks, which, under tighter regulations post-2008, proved more robust. However, new challenges such as inflation, war, and digital disruptions continue to pose threats to economic stability. The global economy has experienced several significant recessions throughout history, many of which were either triggered or exacerbated by the banking sector. From the Great Depression in 1929 to the Global Financial Crisis in 2008, banks have played a pivotal role in shaping the trajectory of economic growth and collapse. Poor regulation, excessive risk-taking, and a lack of transparency have often been at the heart of financial disasters. For instance, in 2008, the collapse of Lehman Brothers symbolized the failure of regulatory oversight and the systemic vulnerabilities within the global banking system. The repercussions were catastrophic: millions of people lost their jobs, homes, and savings. Central banks had to intervene on a massive scale, implementing quantitative easing and slashing interest rates to stabilize markets. More recently, the COVID-19 pandemic tested the resilience of banks, which, under tighter regulations post-2008, proved more robust. However, new challenges such as inflation, war, and digital disruptions continue to pose threats to economic stability. The global economy has experienced several significant recessions throughout history, many of which were either triggered or exacerbated by the banking sector. From the Great Depression in 1929 to the Global Financial Crisis in 2008, banks have played a pivotal role in shaping the trajectory of economic growth and collapse. Poor regulation, excessive risk-taking, and a lack of transparency have often been at the heart of financial disasters. For instance, in 2008, the collapse of Lehman Brothers symbolized the failure of regulatory oversight and the systemic vulnerabilities within the global banking system. The repercussions were catastrophic: millions of people lost their jobs, homes, and savings. Central banks had to intervene on a massive scale, implementing quantitative easing and slashing interest rates to stabilize markets. More recently, the COVID-19 pandemic tested the resilience of banks, which, under tighter regulations post-2008, proved more robust. However, new challenges such as inflation, war, and digital disruptions continue to pose threats to economic stability. The global economy has experienced several significant recessions throughout history, many of which were either triggered or exacerbated by the banking sector. From the Great Depression in 1929 to the Global Financial Crisis in 2008, banks have played a pivotal role in shaping the trajectory of economic growth and collapse. Poor regulation, excessive risk-taking, and a lack of transparency have often been at the heart of financial disasters. For instance, in 2008, the collapse of Lehman Brothers symbolized the failure of regulatory oversight and the systemic vulnerabilities within the global banking system. The repercussions were catastrophic: millions of people lost their jobs, homes, and savings. Central banks had to intervene on a massive scale, implementing quantitative easing and slashing interest rates to stabilize markets. More recently, the COVID-19 pandemic tested the resilience of banks, which, under tighter regulations post-2008, proved more robust. However, new challenges such as inflation, war, and digital disruptions continue to pose threats to economic stability. The global economy has experienced several significant recessions throughout history, many of which were either triggered or exacerbated by the banking sector. From the Great Depression in 1929 to the Global Financial Crisis in 2008, banks have played a pivotal role in shaping the trajectory of economic growth and collapse. Poor regulation, excessive risk-taking, and a lack of transparency have often been at the heart of financial disasters. For instance, in 2008, the collapse of Lehman Brothers symbolized the failure of regulatory oversight and the systemic vulnerabilities within the global banking system. The repercussions were catastrophic: millions of people lost their jobs, homes, and savings. Central banks had to intervene on a massive scale, implementing quantitative easing and slashing interest rates to stabilize markets. More recently, the COVID-19 pandemic tested the resilience of banks, which, under tighter regulations post-2008, proved more robust. However, new challenges such as inflation, war, and digital disruptions continue to pose threats to economic stability. The global economy has experienced several significant recessions throughout history, many of which were either triggered or exacerbated by the banking sector. From the Great Depression in 1929 to the Global Financial Crisis in 2008, banks have played a pivotal role in shaping the trajectory of economic growth and collapse. Poor regulation, excessive risk-taking, and a lack of transparency have often been at the heart of financial disasters. For instance, in 2008, the collapse of Lehman Brothers symbolized the failure of regulatory oversight and the systemic vulnerabilities within the global banking system. The repercussions were catastrophic: millions of people lost their jobs, homes, and savings. Central banks had to intervene on a massive scale, implementing quantitative easing and slashing interest rates to stabilize markets. More recently, the COVID-19 pandemic tested the resilience of banks, which, under tighter regulations post-2008, proved more robust. However, new challenges such as inflation, war, and digital disruptions continue to pose threats to economic stability. The global economy has experienced several significant recessions throughout history, many of which were either triggered or exacerbated by the banking sector. From the Great Depression in 1929 to the Global Financial Crisis in 2008, banks have played a pivotal role in shaping the trajectory of economic growth and collapse. Poor regulation, excessive risk-taking, and a lack of transparency have often been at the heart of financial disasters. For instance, in 2008, the collapse of Lehman Brothers symbolized the failure of regulatory oversight and the systemic vulnerabilities within the global banking system. The repercussions were catastrophic: millions of people lost their jobs, homes, and savings. Central banks had to intervene on a massive scale, implementing quantitative easing and slashing interest rates to stabilize markets. More recently, the COVID-19 pandemic tested the resilience of banks, which, under tighter regulations post-2008, proved more robust. However, new challenges such as inflation, war, and digital disruptions continue to pose threats to economic stability. The global economy has experienced several significant recessions throughout history, many of which were either triggered or exacerbated by the banking sector. From the Great Depression in 1929 to the Global Financial Crisis in 2008, banks have played a pivotal role in shaping the trajectory of economic growth and collapse. Poor regulation, excessive risk-taking, and a lack of transparency have often been at the heart of financial disasters. For instance, in 2008, the collapse of Lehman Brothers symbolized the failure of regulatory oversight and the systemic vulnerabilities within the global banking system. The repercussions were catastrophic: millions of people lost their jobs, homes, and savings. Central banks had to intervene on a massive scale, implementing quantitative easing and slashing interest rates to stabilize markets. More recently, the COVID-19 pandemic tested the resilience of banks, which, under tighter regulations post-2008, proved more robust. However, new challenges such as inflation, war, and digital disruptions continue to pose threats to economic stability. The global economy has experienced several significant recessions throughout history, many of which were either triggered or exacerbated by the banking sector. From the Great Depression in 1929 to the Global Financial Crisis in 2008, banks have played a pivotal role in shaping the trajectory of economic growth and collapse. Poor regulation, excessive risk-taking, and a lack of transparency have often been at the heart of financial disasters. For instance, in 2008, the collapse of Lehman Brothers symbolized the failure of regulatory oversight and the systemic vulnerabilities within the global banking system. The repercussions were catastrophic: millions of people lost their jobs, homes, and savings. Central banks had to intervene on a massive scale, implementing quantitative easing and slashing interest rates to stabilize markets. More recently, the COVID-19 pandemic tested the resilience of banks, which, under tighter regulations post-2008, proved more robust. However, new challenges such as inflation, war, and digital disruptions continue to pose threats to economic stability. The global economy has experienced several significant recessions throughout history, many of which were either triggered or exacerbated by the banking sector. From the Great Depression in 1929 to the Global Financial Crisis in 2008, banks have played a pivotal role in shaping the trajectory of economic growth and collapse. Poor regulation, excessive risk-taking, and a lack of transparency have often been at the heart of financial disasters. For instance, in 2008, the collapse of Lehman Brothers symbolized the failure of regulatory oversight and the systemic vulnerabilities within the global banking system. The repercussions were catastrophic: millions of people lost their jobs, homes, and savings. Central banks had to intervene on a massive scale, implementing quantitative easing and slashing interest rates to stabilize markets. More recently, the COVID-19 pandemic tested the resilience of banks, which, under tighter regulations post-2008, proved more robust. However, new challenges such as inflation, war, and digital disruptions continue to pose threats to economic stability. The global economy has experienced several significant recessions throughout history, many of which were either triggered or exacerbated by the banking sector. From the Great Depression in 1929 to the Global Financial Crisis in 2008, banks have played a pivotal role in shaping the trajectory of economic growth and collapse. Poor regulation, excessive risk-taking, and a lack of transparency have often been at the heart of financial disasters. For instance, in 2008, the collapse of Lehman Brothers symbolized the failure of regulatory oversight and the systemic vulnerabilities within the global banking system. The repercussions were catastrophic: millions of people lost their jobs, homes, and savings. Central banks had to intervene on a massive scale, implementing quantitative easing and slashing interest rates to stabilize markets. More recently, the COVID-19 pandemic tested the resilience of banks, which, under tighter regulations post-2008, proved more robust. However, new challenges such as inflation, war, and digital disruptions continue to pose threats to economic stability. The global economy has experienced several significant recessions throughout history, many of which were either triggered or exacerbated by the banking sector. From the Great Depression in 1929 to the Global Financial Crisis in 2008, banks have played a pivotal role in shaping the trajectory of economic growth and collapse. Poor regulation, excessive risk-taking, and a lack of transparency have often been at the heart of financial disasters. For instance, in 2008, the collapse of Lehman Brothers symbolized the failure of regulatory oversight and the systemic vulnerabilities within the global banking system. The repercussions were catastrophic: millions of people lost their jobs, homes, and savings. Central banks had to intervene on a massive scale, implementing quantitative easing and slashing interest rates to stabilize markets. More recently, the COVID-19 pandemic tested the resilience of banks, which, under tighter regulations post-2008, proved more robust. However, new challenges such as inflation, war, and digital disruptions continue to pose threats to economic stability. The global economy has experienced several significant recessions throughout history, many of which were either triggered or exacerbated by the banking sector. From the Great Depression in 1929 to the Global Financial Crisis in 2008, banks have played a pivotal role in shaping the trajectory of economic growth and collapse. Poor regulation, excessive risk-taking, and a lack of transparency have often been at the heart of financial disasters. For instance, in 2008, the collapse of Lehman Brothers symbolized the failure of regulatory oversight and the systemic vulnerabilities within the global banking system. The repercussions were catastrophic: millions of people lost their jobs, homes, and savings. Central banks had to intervene on a massive scale, implementing quantitative easing and slashing interest rates to stabilize markets. More recently, the COVID-19 pandemic tested the resilience of banks, which, under tighter regulations post-2008, proved more robust. However, new challenges such as inflation, war, and digital disruptions continue to pose threats to economic stability. The global economy has experienced several significant recessions throughout history, many of which were either triggered or exacerbated by the banking sector. From the Great Depression in 1929 to the Global Financial Crisis in 2008, banks have played a pivotal role in shaping the trajectory of economic growth and collapse. Poor regulation, excessive risk-taking, and a lack of transparency have often been at the heart of financial disasters. For instance, in 2008, the collapse of Lehman Brothers symbolized the failure of regulatory oversight and the systemic vulnerabilities within the global banking system. The repercussions were catastrophic: millions of people lost their jobs, homes, and savings. Central banks had to intervene on a massive scale, implementing quantitative easing and slashing interest rates to stabilize markets.

More recently, the COVID-19 pandemic tested the resilience of banks, which, under tighter regulations post-2008, proved more robust. However, new challenges such as inflation, war, and digital disruptions continue to pose threats to economic stability. The global economy has experienced several significant recessions throughout history, many of which were either triggered or exacerbated by the banking sector. From the Great Depression in 1929 to the Global Financial Crisis in 2008, banks have played a pivotal role in shaping the trajectory of economic growth and collapse. Poor regulation, excessive risk-taking, and a lack of transparency have often been at the heart of financial disasters. For instance, in 2008, the collapse of Lehman Brothers symbolized the failure of regulatory oversight and the systemic vulnerabilities within the global banking system. The repercussions were catastrophic: millions of people lost their jobs, homes, and savings. Central banks had to intervene on a massive scale, implementing quantitative easing and slashing interest rates to stabilize markets. More recently, the COVID-19 pandemic tested the resilience of banks, which, under tighter regulations post-2008, proved more robust. However, new challenges such as inflation, war, and digital disruptions continue to pose threats to economic stability. The global economy has experienced several significant recessions throughout history, many of which were either triggered or exacerbated by the banking sector. From the Great Depression in 1929 to the Global Financial Crisis in 2008, banks have played a pivotal role in shaping the trajectory of economic growth and collapse. Poor regulation, excessive risk-taking, and a lack of transparency have often been at the heart of financial disasters. For instance, in 2008, the collapse of Lehman Brothers symbolized the failure of regulatory oversight and the systemic vulnerabilities within the global banking system. The repercussions were catastrophic: millions of people lost their jobs, homes, and savings. Central banks had to intervene on a massive scale, implementing quantitative easing and slashing interest rates to stabilize markets. More recently, the COVID-19 pandemic tested the resilience of banks, which, under tighter regulations post-2008, proved more robust. However, new challenges such as inflation, war, and digital disruptions continue to pose threats to economic stability. The global economy has experienced several significant recessions throughout history, many of which were either triggered or exacerbated by the banking sector. From the Great Depression in 1929 to the Global Financial Crisis in 2008, banks have played a pivotal role in shaping the trajectory of economic growth and collapse. Poor regulation, excessive risk-taking, and a lack of transparency have often been at the heart of financial disasters. For instance, in 2008, the collapse of Lehman Brothers symbolized the failure of regulatory oversight and the systemic vulnerabilities within the global banking system. The repercussions were catastrophic: millions of people lost their jobs, homes, and savings. Central banks had to intervene on a massive scale, implementing quantitative easing and slashing interest rates to stabilize markets. More recently, the COVID-19 pandemic tested the resilience of banks, which, under tighter regulations post-2008, proved more robust. However, new challenges such as inflation, war, and digital disruptions continue to pose threats to economic stability. The global economy has experienced several significant recessions throughout history, many of which were either triggered or exacerbated by the banking sector. From the Great Depression in 1929 to the Global Financial Crisis in 2008, banks have played a pivotal role in shaping the trajectory of economic growth and collapse. Poor regulation, excessive risk-taking, and a lack of transparency have often been at the heart of financial disasters. For instance, in 2008, the collapse of Lehman Brothers symbolized the failure of regulatory oversight and the systemic vulnerabilities within the global banking system. The repercussions were catastrophic: millions of people lost their jobs, homes, and savings. Central banks had to intervene on a massive scale, implementing quantitative easing and slashing interest rates to stabilize markets. More recently, the COVID-19 pandemic tested the resilience of banks, which, under tighter regulations post-2008, proved more robust. However, new challenges such as inflation, war, and digital disruptions continue to pose threats to economic stability. The global economy has experienced several significant recessions throughout history, many of which were either triggered or exacerbated by the banking sector. From the Great Depression in 1929 to the Global

Financial Crisis in 2008, banks have played a pivotal role in shaping the trajectory of economic growth and collapse. Poor regulation, excessive risk-taking, and a lack of transparency have often been at the heart of financial disasters. For instance, in 2008, the collapse of Lehman Brothers symbolized the failure of regulatory oversight and the systemic vulnerabilities within the global banking system. The repercussions were catastrophic: millions of people lost their jobs, homes, and savings. Central banks had to intervene on a massive scale, implementing quantitative easing and slashing interest rates to stabilize markets. More recently, the COVID-19 pandemic tested the resilience of banks, which, under tighter regulations post-2008, proved more robust. However, new challenges such as inflation, war, and digital disruptions continue to pose threats to economic stability.

www.ingramcontent.com/pod-product-compliance
Lightning Source LLC
Chambersburg PA
CBHW040209110726
48005CB00019B/2952